I0569373

WHITNEY STONE

Fine, I'll Heal

A No-BS Guide to Healing for the Stubborn, Skeptical, and Slightly Over It

For the version of me who survived without a manual—here's the one I wish you had."

I didn't write this because I figured it all out. I wrote this because I was drowning, no one else was handing out life jackets, and I got tired of pretending I knew how to swim. This book is the one I needed thrown to me. Because every day is a new beginning—and some of us are rebuilding the damn boat while still waist-deep in the water.

— WHITNEY STONE

Contents

Preface

If you're holding this book, you're probably tired. Like, soul-exhausted. Not "I need a nap" tired—"if one more person tells me to try breathwork, I might scream into a potholder" tired.

The kind of tired that comes from carrying invisible sh*t for years. From masking pain with productivity. From being everyone's emotional support human while quietly unraveling one anxious thought at a time. You've smiled when you wanted to scream. Nodded when you wanted to run. Held it together when what you really needed was someone to say, "Hey, it makes sense you're falling apart."

This book is for you.

It's not a memoir—though my story's all over these pages like trauma glitter. And it's not a clinical manual—though there's more psychology here than your group chat's seen since someone rage-texted about their ex in all caps. *Fine, I'll Heal* is what I needed when I was sick of the self-help section but still knew I couldn't keep living like a walking, talking nervous system flare-up.

It's raw. It's real. And yes, it swears. Sometimes creatively.

This isn't about fixing yourself into a shiny new version of "healed." It's about dragging your beautifully chaotic self to the table, laying out the mess, and saying, "Okay… now what?" With curiosity. With grit. And with enough humor to survive the hard parts.

I wrote this for the spiral moments. The shutdowns. The days when healing feels like a scam and emotional regulation feels like a dare. Inside, you'll find tools that actually work when you're knee-deep in the wreckage—not just when the sun is shining and your affirmations are hitting.

So take what lands. Leave what doesn't. And if something punches you in the soul—don't worry. That was intentional.

Let's begin.

Acknowledgments

The messy middle wouldn't have meant anything without you.

To Josh

You made me question everything I thought I knew—and that was the beginning of everything. Loving you cracked me open in all the best and hardest ways. You taught me to fight harder, listen deeper, and finally trust my gut—even when the world said I was wrong. You've always been worth the battle. You still are. Watching you navigate life with your strength and humor reminds me why I never gave up.

To Aniah

You are light and clarity and beauty, all wrapped in fierce bravery. You've been a mirror, a motivator, and—on the hardest days—the reason I kept going. Watching you become exactly who you are is one of the greatest honors of my life. You remind me every single day that softness is not weakness—it's superpower.

To the therapists

The ones who didn't gaslight me, misdiagnose me, or make me feel like a human red flag wrapped in warning tape—you're the reason I kept trying. You're rare. Thank you for doing the work *and* doing it with humanity.

To Katie

We've been living slightly different chapters from the same book—and somehow still managed to highlight each other's margins. Thank you for the honesty, the humor, and the healing that came from knowing I wasn't alone in the plot twists.

To Sara

My best friend, emotional anchor, and honorary mom. You saw me clearly when I was still trying to disappear. You've been the soft place, the safe place, and the sass when I forgot who the hell I was. Thank you for all of it.

To the Saints community I never knew I needed

I didn't know friendships like this existed—the kind where you're accepted just because you *are*, not because you earned it. Thank you for showing up, cheering loud, and making space for my family like we belonged before we even believed it ourselves. You've redefined what community means to me.

To my Self-Doubt Part

You questioned every sentence, second-guessed every truth, and whispered just loud enough to make me hesitate. But here's the thing: you also made me sharper. You forced me to dig deeper, clarify what mattered, and stand by my voice even when it shook. You kept things spicy, sure—but you also made this more honest.

To my Over-Responsible Manager

You held this entire book together with duct tape and caffeine. You wrote chapters in your sleep, planned edits in the shower, and refused to drop a single ball—even when it was crushing you. You kept showing up like the whole world depended on it. I see you. I love you. You've earned your rest.

To the healing community

You're the quiet force behind every brave step I've taken. The ones who showed me that healing doesn't have to be perfect to be powerful. You gave me language when I had none, tools when I felt broken, and proof that being a mess doesn't disqualify you from growth—it makes you real. Thank you for lighting the path when I couldn't see my own.

To everyone who contributed to my pain

You were the fire I had to walk through to write this book. Your silence, your betrayal, your denial—it all left a mark. And while I won't pretend to thank you for the damage, I will thank myself for surviving it. You are part of the story. But you don't get the final word. I do.

And finally...

To every person who ever called me *too sensitive, too much, too emotional*, or *too intense*—

Turns out, all that "too much" made for one hell of a voice. I wrote the book you didn't think I could. The one you probably need therapy for. And

I'm not even sorry.

To you, the reader

Thank you for picking up this book—and staying with it through the hard parts, the tender parts, and the *wait, is she dragging me?* parts. Whether you read it in one sitting or dog-eared it over months, you let my story hold a mirror to your own—and that's brave as hell.

You didn't have to open this book. You didn't have to keep going. But you did. And I hope somewhere in these pages, you felt seen, validated, or at the very least, a little less alone.

You are not broken. You are becoming. And if this book helped you remember that, even just once, then it did exactly what it was meant to do.

Keep going.

I'm rooting for you.

Introduction

If you're here, odds are you've hit that special flavor of burnout where even self-help books feel exhausting. You're juggling bills, relationships, existential dread, and possibly a child screaming over the wrong color cup. You don't need another "just meditate" solution—you need something real. Something that works in the Target parking lot when your nervous system is staging a coup.

That's this book.

It's part personal story, part psychological deep-dive, and part survival manual for humans who are trying to heal while still dealing with, well... *life*. It's for the ones who never got the luxury of pausing everything to go find themselves in Bali. It's for the ones doing the work between school drop-offs, trauma flashbacks, and reheated coffee.

Credentials? Sort of.

Not a therapist. Just deeply obsessed.

I'm not a licensed therapist (*yet*), but I've spent years deep in the trenches of trauma recovery—both personally and academically. I've devoured everything I could find on IFS, DBT, attachment theory, nervous system regulation, and how not to emotionally implode at the worst possible moment.

This book is what happens when lived experience meets research-backed insight and decides to tell the truth. No jargon. No sugarcoating. No pretending healing is always a candlelit journaling session. Sometimes it's crying in your car while Googling "what to do when your fight-or-flight won't turn off."

1

Read This However You Need

There's no gold star for healing in order.

This book wasn't designed to be read straight through like a textbook. Start wherever you want. Skip the parts that feel too raw. Dog-ear the pages you'll pretend you'll come back to. This isn't linear healing—it's pick-your-own-adventure therapy for the emotionally exhausted.

Some chapters might punch you in the soul. Some might feel like a warm hug. Either way, if it hits—good. That means it matters. Take what lands, leave the rest, and remind yourself that you don't have to be *ready* to begin. You just have to begin.

Healing Disclaimer

Because I'd rather give you a trigger warning than false hope.

This book talks about trauma, addiction, grief, abuse, mental health, and all the messy middle parts most people try to skip. Some of it might be hard to read. Some of it might hit too close. That's okay. Close the book. Come back later. Or don't. Your pace is sacred. Your nervous system is not on anyone else's timeline.

Also: this is not therapy. This is not a substitute for therapy. If you're struggling, please reach out to a qualified mental health professional. You deserve real support. Full stop.

Self-Published, Slightly Unhinged, Still Worth Reading

Formatting quirks brought to you by healing at 2 a.m.

Yes, this book is self-published. That means I did the writing, editing, layout, proofreading, existential spiraling, and probably missed a comma somewhere along the way. If your copy has a wonky margin or rogue typo... congrats, it's now a collector's item with *emotional texture*.

2

I

Part 1: The Journey

Tracing the Wreckage So You Can Rebuild on Purpose
This is where it gets messy. Welcome to the emotional crime scene
where your coping skills were born. We'll piece together the
"WTF is wrong with me?" puzzle and untangle how your nervous
system, trauma history, and attachment style shaped your
survival.
It's not pretty—but it's necessary.

Congratulations, You're Officially Over It

The "Why Now?" Meltdown That Turned Into a Healing Journey

So, here you are—standing in the middle of your life, staring at the metaphorical wreckage like you just woke up in the aftermath of a hurricane you don't remember signing up for.

You've got questions—big ones.

Why do I react the way I do? Why am I like this? And, most hauntingly: *Is this just who I am, or did something break along the way?*

This is where healing starts.

Not the fluffy, buy-a-crystal-and-journal-about-gratitude kind.

The *oh shit* kind—the kind where you realize you've been in survival mode for so long you don't actually know who you'd be without it.

You've been holding it together with duct tape, hypervigilance, and a suspicious amount of caffeine—and suddenly, your system is like, *yeah... we're done here.*

Welcome.

You've reached the part of the story where pretending everything's fine just isn't cutting it anymore.

You're officially over it.

And that's exactly where you're supposed to be.

The "WTF Happened To Me?" Moment

(The Meltdown You Didn't Schedule but Definitely Needed)

Everyone who stumbles their way into a healing journey gets here the same way: by running out of coping mechanisms that still work.

For some, it's a full-blown breakdown. For others, it's subtler—like realizing you can't relax without spiraling into a shame-fueled existential crisis.

For me? It was the emotional gymnastics. The over-explaining. The scanning people's faces for tone shifts like I was running airport-level security. The compulsive need to manage everyone else's emotions while having no clue how to regulate my own.

Once I saw it, I couldn't unsee it. I wasn't just "intense." I wasn't "too sensitive." I was a walking trauma response with a decent wardrobe and a good sense of humor.

Naturally, I did what any over-functioning, hyper-aware adult does: I tried to logic my way out of it.

Spoiler: That didn't work. Because here's the thing—

Self-awareness alone doesn't heal you.

It just makes you painfully aware that you *need* healing.

Emotional Fragmentation 101

(Or, Why You Feel Like 12 People Arguing in a Trench Coat)

What you're experiencing isn't just burnout, mood swings, or poor time management (though, sure—same). It's emotional fragmentation: the very real experience of living in pieces.

Different versions of you show up in different moments, often with completely conflicting goals. One part of you wants connection. Another is scanning the exit for safety threats. One wants to open up. Another would rather chew glass than trust someone.

IFS—Internal Family Systems therapy—calls these parts. And no, it's not woo-woo. It's actually one of the most grounded, compassionate ways to understand how your brain learned to survive what it couldn't control.

These parts aren't the enemy. They're the overworked crew that kept your ship afloat through the worst storms—

They just don't know the storm is over.

What This Book Is (And What It Isn't)

(A No-Bullshit Guide to Healing, Self-Trust, and Untangling the Wreckage)

Let me be clear: this book isn't going to sell you the fantasy of "healing" as a soft-focus Instagram glow-up.

You won't find me preaching toxic positivity or acting like shadow work is a weekend hobby.

What you *will* find is a brutally honest, occasionally sarcastic, deeply practical guide to untangling the mess you didn't ask for—but inherited, absorbed, and survived anyway.

We'll talk trauma, survival parts, shame, boundaries, fear, trust, and the complicated art of actually living after years of just getting through.

You'll meet the internal characters running your emotional life. You'll learn how to rewire your nervous system without feeling like a self-help zombie. And you'll do it all in a way that doesn't require you to be someone you're not.

Wreckage Control: Soul CPR for When You've Just Dug Through the Rubble

(Because reading about healing is cute—but doing it is where the magic (and mess) happens.)

You just waded through the emotional wreckage of your survival system like the badass archaeologist of your own trauma timeline. Don't leave the site without grabbing a few tools. These aren't deep dives—they're gentle reconnections. Think of them as emotional cool-downs before you take on the next dragon.

Name Your Wreckage

7

List out the parts of you still stuck in survival mode.

Examples: The people-pleaser. The ghoster. The mind-reading overfunctioner.

These aren't flaws. They're receipts—proof of how hard you worked to stay safe in systems that didn't.

Try a Part Mapping Check-In

Draw a circle. Write *Me* in the middle. Surround it with the emotional roles that hijack the wheel in different settings (The Fixer at work, The Ice Queen during conflict, etc.).

You're not judging. You're just noticing the internal group chat.

Offer Compassion to One Part

Pick a survival part and write it a quick note. No poetic monologue needed.

Something like: *Hey. I know you were trying to help. I see you. You don't have to carry this alone anymore.*

Yes, you're writing to yourself. No, it's not weird. It's healing.

Next Up: Why I Don't Trust Anyone (Including Myself)

So now you've met the wreckage. You've mapped the parts. You've maybe even written a love letter to your inner chaos coordinator. But there's one thing we haven't talked about yet—and it's kind of a dealbreaker when it comes to healing: **trust.** Or, more accurately, the complete and utter lack of it.

Because it's one thing to realize you've been living in survival mode. It's another to admit you don't even trust yourself to do it any differently.

Let's talk about the trust issues you didn't ask for—but definitely inherited.

Why I Don't Trust Anyone (Including Myself)

When your brain learns to survive instead of connect.

Trigger Warning

This chapter discusses trauma, childhood neglect, sexual assault, and the fallout of false reporting. If any of these feel like too much right now, honor that. Skip, skim, or set this down. You don't owe anyone your re-exposure. Your healing is valid—even when it moves at a crawl.

Rebuilding After Betrayal & Neglect

How self-reliance becomes armor when connection fails.

If you've ever been called guarded, too independent, or difficult to get close to, I can almost guarantee you didn't just wake up one morning and think, *"You know what sounds fun? Emotional isolation."*

You *learned* it.

The way some kids learn piano, you learned how to rely on no one—because every time you did, they either vanished, failed you, or handed you the kind of disappointment that turns your stomach into concrete. So eventually, your nervous system made an executive decision:

Depending on people is a liability.

You might not even remember making that call. It just happened. One day you realized you don't tell people when you're spiraling. You ask for help only when you're in DEFCON 1. And when someone says, *"I love you,"* you start pre-mourning the inevitable abandonment like you're prepping for a breakup that hasn't even happened yet.

You didn't just stop trusting people.

You stopped trusting yourself.

The Origins of Your Survival Patterns

The childhood shift from "seen" to "invisible."

I remember the exact moment my nervous system filed vulnerability under *"hell no."* I was thirteen when my adoptive parents—who believed they couldn't have biological children—suddenly could. Surprise! And just like that, I was emotionally evicted. From center stage to stagehand.

When my sister was born with a chromosome disorder, everything shifted. Hospital visits, emergencies, survival mode. I understood it. But I also internalized it. No one ever said, *"Hey Whitney, I know this is hard on you too."* I became an emotional orphan in my own house.

So I did what every high-functioning, invisibly hurting kid does:

I held it together. I performed. I tried to be useful.

And then... she died.

Once the funeral ended, so did any illusion that someone might check in on me. I snapped. Hard. I went full rebellion, lit the match, and watched it burn.

When Desperation Meets Trauma

What happens when no one protects the protector.

That desperation led me places I shouldn't have been.

At 14, I was sexually assaulted. And even in my own trauma, I was still trying to protect everyone *but* me.

I told the police what happened—then immediately panicked. I didn't

10

want him to "get in real trouble." His sister threatened me. I folded like wet paper. I wrote him a note saying I had lied, just to keep the fallout manageable.

That note? It sealed everything.

Suddenly, I wasn't the scared girl anymore—I was "the liar." The system didn't care why I wrote it. No one asked *what happened before*. I got charged with false reporting. Everyone disappeared. I was left carrying a narrative that wasn't even mine.

That was the day my nervous system tattooed a new rule on my soul:

You're on your own. No one is coming.

Becoming the Fixer

How overfunctioning became your love language.

I didn't just stop trusting people—I went full fortress. Shut down. Armored up. And when all that rage and grief finally burned out, I did the only thing I could think of:

I made myself indispensable.

If I couldn't be loved for who I was, maybe I could be *needed*. If I could anticipate what people wanted before they said it—maybe they'd stay. Maybe I'd matter. So I became the fixer. The emotional support human. The one who never needed help, because needing help had only ever led to pain.

I held it all together. And quietly fell apart.

The Truth About Trust Issues

It's not just fear—it's strategy.

When people say *"I have trust issues,"* they usually mean they're afraid of getting hurt.

But trust issues aren't just fear of betrayal. They're the hypervigilance behind every over-explanation. They're the reason you apologize for having needs. They're the voice in your head that whispers, *"They'll leave if you mess this up."*

11

Trust issues show up like this:

- Overfunctioning because love feels conditional.
- Hyper-independence disguised as strength.
- Reassurance-seeking dressed up as responsibility.
- A deep, persistent belief that if people *really* knew you... they'd bail.

You're not broken.
You're strategic.
And your brain has the receipts to prove it.

Rebuilding Trust

When your brain thinks that's a terrible idea.

You can't just wake up one day and say, *"You know what? I'm gonna trust again!"* That's adorable. But no.

Trust isn't a logic problem. It's a *felt* experience. And if your nervous system is wired for chronic self-doubt or skepticism, it's not going to drop its armor just because you gave it a pep talk.

Here's what it actually takes:

- **Start with micro-trust.**
  Forget dramatic acts of vulnerability. Can someone show up on time? Keep a promise? Text back? That's where trust starts—not with confessions, but with consistency.
- **Practice self-trust.**
  Validate your own decisions, even when they're small. Say, *"I made a choice. That counts."* Your nervous system needs proof that you're safe in your own hands.
- **Spot the trauma masquerading as independence.**
  "I don't need anyone" sounds cool. But most of the time, it's just a fancy way of saying, *"I've been hurt too many damn times."*

Micro Moves for the Trust-Deprived

Because rebuilding trust doesn't start with a leap—it starts with a toe in the water.

You don't have to overhaul your entire emotional infrastructure to start trusting again. That's not how any of this works. Trust isn't declared—it's earned, slowly, in the smallest moments. These tools won't demand much, but they might shift everything.

Rebuild trust in micro-moments

Pick one decision you made this week. Any decision. Name it. Own it. That's self-trust. Doesn't matter if it was picking the right lane at Target or finally hitting "send" on the text you've been avoiding.

Name the old script

Fill in the blanks:

"If I trust people, then _____."

"If I trust myself, then _____."

Whatever your brain blurts out? That's the fear behind the freeze. Start there.

Let someone show up for you—on purpose

Ask for something low-stakes. A check-in. A ride. A snack run. Letting people in slowly still counts. You're not building a drawbridge overnight—you're cracking the door. That's enough.

Final Thought:

Trust issues aren't a defect. They're a defense. They're a nervous system strategy wrapped in a lifetime of disappointments. But once you start seeing them for what they *are*—learned patterns, not personal failings—you can stop blaming yourself for the way you survived.

And that's when the real healing begins.

Next Up: How You Became a Walking Defense Mechanism

Because of course you're guarded. You didn't get that way by accident. You didn't wake up one day and decide to become hypervigilant, emotionally armored, or allergic to intimacy just for fun. That sh*t was built—brick by brick—out of disappointments, betrayals, gaslighting, and a thousand little moments where your needs were too big, your feelings were too much, or your voice was met with silence.

You didn't become a walking defense mechanism because you're dramatic. You became one because you learned—early and often—that staying open wasn't safe. So your brain got creative. Your nervous system adapted. And your personality became a survival strategy.

Let's talk about that.

How You Became a Walking Defense Mechanism

Relaxed? No. Expertly Armored? Absolutely.

(Why You're Not Broken—Just Brilliantly Conditioned)

Let's get one thing straight: you're not broken. You're not doomed to sabotage every relationship, and you're not destined to live in a perpetual state of *Do they actually like me, or am I just annoying?*

What you are, though, is a walking, talking bundle of defense mechanisms—carefully crafted by your nervous system, shaped by your environment, and reinforced every time life threw another curveball at your head.

And here's the kicker: you didn't choose this. No one wakes up and says, *"You know what sounds fun? Constantly overanalyzing every relationship while my nervous system ping-pongs between craving connection and bracing for abandonment!"*

This is what happens when your brain and body adapt to unpredictable environments. Your attachment style, trust issues, and knee-jerk reactions to intimacy (or the terrifying void of it) aren't just emotional struggles. They're neurological survival strategies.

The good news? These patterns are not permanent.

Just like your nervous system learned to protect you in ways that kept you safe (but also stuck), it can also learn that safety and connection are not

15

mutually exclusive.

The Science of Pushing People Away (or Clinging Too Tightly)

(Your Nervous System Isn't Being Dramatic—It's Doing Its Job)

If you've ever spiraled over an unanswered text, felt a pit in your stomach when someone took too long to reply, or—on the flip side—felt physically suffocated when someone actually met your emotional needs (*because what is this, sorcery?*)...

Congratulations: your nervous system is just trying to keep you safe.

Safe from what, exactly?

Oh, just the entire history of human connection that your brain has cataloged and weaponized against you.

How Your Nervous System Decides What's "Safe"

Predictable > Healthy, Every Time

Here's the thing: attachment isn't about what's *healthy*—it's about what's *predictable*. Your nervous system doesn't care if your relationship is secure. It cares if it feels familiar.

So, if you grew up in an environment where:

- Love was inconsistent
- Affection had strings attached
- Your needs were chronically ignored

...your brain didn't just *think* something was wrong—it *felt* it. And it adapted the only way it knew how:

- If people were unreliable, you learned to cling harder. (Hello, anxious attachment.)
- If love was conditional, you learned to earn it. (Cue people-pleasing and emotional labor Olympics.)

- If closeness brought pain, you braced for the worst. (Pre-rejecting yourself to feel in control? Classic.)
- If you were really lucky (read: deeply confused), you did all of the above. (*Welcome to disorganized attachment.*)

Attachment Styles: The Nervous System's Pre-Programmed Defense Strategies

(It's Not You—It's Your Settings)

Think of your attachment style as your nervous system's default mode in relationships. Some people? They're out here running Secure 2.0 like it's factory-installed.

The rest of us? We've been glitching since childhood and covering it with sarcasm.

Let's break it down:

Anxious Attachment

Your nervous system is always on edge, scanning for signs of disconnection. You overthink, overfunction, and sometimes overstay—because closeness feels like safety, but its potential disappearance feels like death.

Avoidant Attachment

Your system learned that vulnerability = danger. You crave connection, but not at the cost of control. So you stay independent, guarded, and a little bit emotionally MIA.

Disorganized Attachment

You are the walking contradiction. You want closeness and distance. You push and pull. Your nervous system doesn't know if it's supposed to run toward love or duck for cover.

17

Secure Attachment

You believe people are dependable, your needs are valid, and closeness isn't a threat.

Must be nice.

I didn't start here. I lived in the anxious-avoidant push-pull cycle for years—craving connection while bracing for betrayal. But once I learned my nervous system wasn't broken, just misinformed, everything started to shift.

Rewriting the Script: Teaching Your Nervous System a New Story

Your Attachment Style Is a Habit, Not a Life Sentence

Your attachment style isn't your identity—it's your nervous system's training manual. And it *can* be rewritten.

Here's how:

- Notice the pattern before you react.
  Ask yourself: Is this about what's happening now—or what happened then?
- Regulate first, respond second.
  Breathe. Move. Ground. Your body needs to feel safe before it can do anything rational.
- Practice secure behaviors—even when they feel wrong.If you're anxious, pause before seeking reassurance.If you're avoidant, stay emotionally present.
  If you're disorganized, notice when you send mixed signals—and try to soften into clarity.
- Teach your body that connection can be safe.
  Real healing happens in safe relationships. Repetition, consistency, and nervous system regulation—not just insight—change the game.

De-Armoring 101: How to Soften Without Surrendering

If you're ready. No pressure.

This chapter cracked open the blueprint of your emotional armor—the habits, the shutdowns, the ghosting with a side of guilt. You're not fragile. You're fortified. But maybe it's time to see what's underneath the scaffolding. These tools are here to help you notice, not fix. Clarity first. Change comes later.

1. Identify Your Default Armor

Complete this sentence: *"When I feel unsafe in relationships, I usually _____."*

Maybe you shut down. Maybe you apologize for having needs. Maybe you ghost like it's your full-time job. There's no shame here—just data. This is your nervous system doing what it was trained to do: protect you.

2. Track a Pattern Without Judgment

For one day—or one interaction—just watch what your system does. Ask yourself:

Is this person actually unsafe... or is this an old fear in new clothes?

Am I seeking reassurance or bracing for rejection?

What does my body feel like right now?

You're not changing anything yet. You're just witnessing. And witnessing is its own kind of healing.

3. Choose One Secure Behavior to Practice

Pick one. Just one.

Wait 20 minutes before sending that anxious follow-up text.

Accept comfort without cracking a joke or pushing it away.

Stay present during conflict without self-abandoning for the win.

You're not betraying your defenses—you're expanding your options. That's growth.

19

Reminder:
Your patterns made sense. They got you through.
But you're allowed to outgrow what helped you survive.
You don't have to stop protecting yourself.
You just don't have to do it alone anymore.

Because your emotional armor wasn't random—it was custom-built by a younger you who didn't have better options. But what happens to the parts of you that got buried underneath it? The ones that weren't just protected... they were silenced?

Next Up: The Part of You That's Still Waiting to Be Heard

(When Silence Was the Only Safe Option)
So now you know—your attachment style isn't a flaw. It's a roadmap your nervous system drew, using trauma as the compass and survival as the destination.

But there's one part we haven't talked about yet.

The version of you who couldn't fight. Who couldn't flee. Who couldn't fix it. The part that didn't armor up—because she didn't even get the chance.

She just disappeared.

Not because she wanted to. Because no one was listening anyway.

It's time to find her.

Not to drag her into the spotlight or force her to speak—but to sit beside her in the dark and whisper, *"I see you. And I'm not leaving this time."*

The Part of You That's Still Waiting to Be Heard

When Silence Becomes a Survival Strategy

(Why some parts of us stop speaking before we ever learn how to scream)

Imagine standing in a glass box in the middle of a crowded room. You can see everyone. You can hear everything. But no one sees you. You bang on the walls. You scream. You wave your arms. Nothing. They keep talking, laughing, moving around you like you're not even there.

At first, you panic. You shout louder. Maybe you even throw yourself against the glass, hoping somebody will notice. But they don't. So eventually... you stop trying. You sit down. You go quiet. You tell yourself that being invisible is better than being ignored.

That's what it felt like to be thirteen years old in my house. That's what it felt like when my sister was born and my entire world shifted without my consent. That's what it felt like when she died—and I realized no one was going to check on me. That's what it felt like when I was sexually assaulted and, instead of protection, I was given punishment.

At some point, I stopped trying to be seen. I stopped believing that being heard was even an option. And that's how I ended up trapped in the glass box—watching, waiting, disappearing into the background.

How I Learned to Make Myself Invisible

(The slow, quiet descent into silence)

I didn't wake up one day and decide to shrink myself into nothingness. That's not how survival patterns work. They don't arrive with a dramatic monologue and a neon sign that says, "This is your new coping mechanism!" They creep in. Quietly. Gradually. They disguise themselves as logic. As strength. As being easy to deal with.

For me, it started with small things. I learned that when my parents were stressed about my sister, they had less patience for me. So I tried to make things easier. I became the responsible one. The self-sufficient one. The kid who didn't add to the weight they were already carrying. But even before that, I had already learned what it felt like to be an afterthought.

I was adopted as a baby—raised in a home I was told was mine, but one that never truly felt like I belonged in it. My mom told me, "We chose you," as if that should make me feel special. But all I heard was the unspoken reality underneath: You weren't ours to begin with. Being chosen wasn't the same as being inevitable. It wasn't the same as belonging.

So I grew up trying to prove I was worth keeping. Worth noticing. Worth holding onto. Worth being.

The Impact of Not Being Believed

(Sexual Assault & Self-Trust Fractures)

The thing about living in a glass box is that it doesn't just keep people from seeing you—it slowly erodes your ability to trust what you see. After my sister died—after months of screaming inside my own head while my parents grieved around me but never *with* me—I finally found someone who seemed to see me. Or at least, I thought I did. At first, his attention felt like safety. Like proof that I mattered. That I existed. That someone had finally noticed the quiet girl behind the glass.

But that illusion didn't last. What started as validation turned into something that shattered me. And when I finally gathered the courage

22

to speak up—to say out loud, *This happened to me*—I was met with a truth more devastating than the harm itself: being hurt and being believed are not the same thing.

No one protected me. No one comforted me. No one said, *You didn't deserve this.* Instead, I was punished. Labeled a liar. Charged with false reporting. That was the moment my nervous system learned a new rule it would follow for years: silence is safer than the truth.

Because how do you trust yourself again when the world insists your reality isn't real? How do you believe your own experiences when the people who were supposed to protect you decide your pain is inconvenient? I learned—through silence, through betrayal, through punishment—that speaking up didn't bring healing. It brought more hurt.

So I stopped. I stopped trusting myself. I stopped believing what I knew. I stopped living outside the walls I had built. The glass box wasn't just a prison. It became the only place that felt remotely safe.

IFS Insight: The Part of Me Still Locked Away

(Why thirteen still feels like yesterday)

Even now, there's a part of me that still lives—trapped—in that glass box. She's about thirteen. She doesn't say much, but she watches everything. She doesn't trust easily. She assumes abandonment before it happens. She braces for people to leave the second they get too close. And honestly? I don't blame her.

She learned the hard way that being seen doesn't mean being protected. She learned that people can look right at you and still decide you don't matter.

Internal Family Systems (IFS) teaches us that these parts of ourselves—the ones stuck in trauma, the ones still waiting to be heard—aren't broken. They don't need to be fixed. They don't need to be discarded. They just need us to listen.

Because here's the truth: That thirteen-year-old version of me—the one who got shoved to the sidelines, the one who wasn't checked on, the one

23

who decided being invisible was safer than being real—she wasn't wrong. She did what she had to do to survive.

And now, it's my job to go back and sit with her. To let her know she doesn't have to scream to be heard. That she's not a problem to be solved. That she was real. That she does matter. That I see her now. And that, finally—she can step outside the glass box.

Final Thought

(To the ones still screaming silently)

If you ever feel like you're screaming into the void—like no one hears you, like you've spent your whole life waiting for someone to notice you—just know this: You are not invisible. The world may have failed to see you before. But you can see you now. And that? That changes everything.

Calling in the Ghost Part

The version of you that disappeared didn't choose silence. It just didn't feel safe speaking up.

There's a part of you still behind the glass—quiet, guarded, maybe completely shut down. Not broken. Not dramatic. Just done being ignored. This isn't about dragging that part into the light. It's about pulling up a chair outside the box so they know they're not alone in there anymore.

1. Write to the Invisible Part of You

No therapist voice. No "healed self" monologue. Just honesty.

Try this: *"I know you've been waiting. I know you're tired. I'm here now. I see you."*

This isn't a script—it's a reconnection.

2. Let Your Body Speak First

That invisible part might not use words. It might show up as jaw tension, random tears, or that weird sensation of being thirteen again for no logical reason.

Put one hand over your heart, the other on your stomach. Breathe slow. Ask:

"What part of me is asking to be seen right now?"

You're not looking for a clear answer. You're building trust.

3. Try Mirror Work (The Brave Kind)

Face a mirror. Hold your own gaze—even if it feels awkward.

Say: *"You're not invisible. I see you. You matter. You didn't make this up."*

Say it until it starts to feel less like a performance and more like a possibility.

> **Reminder:**
> Being ignored doesn't mean you were unworthy.
> And being invisible was never your fault.

Next Up: But I Don't Even Feel Anything?

(What happens after you find the quiet part—and there's still nothing there)

You've found the part of you that went quiet. You've sat beside her in the glass box. You've realized she wasn't broken—just silenced. But now there's a new problem: You're finally ready to listen... and there's nothing there. No anger. No sadness. No tears. Just static. Just blankness. Just a body that forgot how to feel because it was too damn dangerous for too damn long.

If you've ever wondered, "Why can't I feel anything?"—this one's for you.

But I Don't Even Feel Anything?

Ah, Emotional Numbness—The Ultimate Party Trick of the Traumatized

(When not feeling anything starts to feel like your only skill set)

I used to think numbness was my superpower. While everyone else was out here crying over minor inconveniences, I was the picture of composure. Stoic. Rational. Unbothered. And, as it turns out, **completely full of shit**. Because here's the truth: I wasn't above emotions. I wasn't some enlightened being who had transcended human suffering. I was disconnected from myself. Numbness wasn't strength—it was a trauma response. And I didn't realize that until my life imploded.

The Freeze Response Disguised as Strength

(Autopilot looks productive until you crash)

When my parents took guardianship of my kids, I didn't collapse into grief like a movie character would. I didn't sob on the kitchen floor or dramatically wail into a throw pillow. Nope—I went full autopilot. My brain short-circuited and decided, *Nah, we're not dealing with this.* Instead, I numbed out—first emotionally, then chemically. Because why stop at one coping mechanism when you can double down?

Alcohol? Absolutely. Drugs? Sure. Keeping myself too busy to think? Obviously. I used whatever it took to keep those feelings locked in a box marked: *DO NOT OPEN UNDER ANY CIRCUMSTANCES.* If I didn't feel anything, then none of it could really hurt me, right?

Spoiler alert: that's not how it works. You can only shove emotions into a box for so long before the box breaks. And when it does? Everything comes flying out at once—like a haunted jack-in-the-box of unprocessed trauma, set to the soundtrack of your own nervous breakdown.

The Myth of Emotional Detachment

(Intellectualizing isn't healing—it's hiding)

My other go-to move was intellectualizing the hell out of everything. I became a walking psychology textbook, analyzing every emotion to death before it even had a chance to surface. If I could name it, define it, chart its origin story, I could hold it at arm's length. That way, I wasn't avoiding my feelings—I was just being logical. Smart. In control.

Except emotional numbness isn't control. It's survival mode. It's the freeze response dressed up as *I'm just not that emotional.* It's your nervous system deciding that feeling is too damn dangerous, so it slams the emergency brake.

And here's the science part: when the body perceives overwhelm as too much to fight or flee from, it hits that emergency brake—and that's your freeze response. It's not laziness. It's not apathy. It's your nervous system putting you on airplane mode.

I didn't know it then, but I had been operating like this since childhood. Growing up in an environment where emotions weren't exactly welcome, I learned quickly that expressing them got me nowhere—so I stopped. I thought detachment was strength. Turns out, it was just unprocessed trauma wearing a very convincing disguise.

When You Don't Feel Anything—Until You Feel Everything

(Spoiler: The emotions always come back)

Here's the thing about emotional numbness: it doesn't last forever. Eventually, the wall cracks. The fog lifts. The feelings come crawling back like stray cats you tried to ignore but accidentally fed once.

For me, that moment didn't come in a therapist's office with ambient music and a box of tissues. It came when I got sober. In 2022, I finally stopped drinking. And suddenly... there was nothing standing between me and the mountain of emotions I'd spent years trying not to feel. No vodka buffer. No chemical escape hatch. No schedule packed tightly enough to outrun the grief. Just me. My body. And a backlog of unfelt emotions, waiting like debt collectors at the door.

I didn't have language for it at first. I just knew I wasn't "fine." I wasn't falling apart either—I was just... unplugged. Like someone had yanked the cord on my emotional power supply. Eventually, I tried to describe it in therapy—the nothingness, the static, the blank disconnection. My therapist looked at me and said, "That's the freeze response."

Not depression. Not apathy. Not weakness. Just my nervous system pulling the emergency brake... for years. And suddenly, it all made sense. I hadn't failed at feeling—I had survived by *not* feeling.

Learning to Actually Feel Again

(Reconnecting without short-circuiting)

When I first heard words like *mindfulness* and *emotional regulation,* my immediate internal response was: *Absolutely not.* Why regulate feelings when you can drown them in vodka and denial?

Sure, those terms are straight out of DBT—and to be fair, I did the DBT thing back in 2013. It gave me structure when I needed it. But that's not what cracked me open in sobriety. This time, it was IFS and brainspotting that helped me feel again. And I don't mean the "just feel your feelings!" fluff from Instagram reels—I mean real tools. The kind that helped me meet the parts of myself that had gone radio silent for years.

IFS gave language to the chaos inside me—the parts that numb out, the ones that push through, the ones that pretend everything's fine. None of them were broken. They were trying. And brainspotting? It gave my body a voice. A way to process grief and trauma without having to make it make sense. Because sometimes healing isn't about understanding—it's about releasing.

That's where I started—not with emotions, but with sensation. Tight shoulders. Nausea. The ever-present jaw clench. If you don't know what you're feeling emotionally, start there. Ask your body. It knows before your brain does. It wasn't a lightbulb moment. It wasn't linear. It felt more like rewiring a house with the power still on—while blindfolded—using emotional duct tape. But every time I checked in with my body, every time I turned toward a part of me I used to avoid, I took a step back toward myself.

Because feeling again isn't about falling apart. It's about finally coming home.

Numbness Isn't Protection—It's a Delay Tactic

(And the interest rate is brutal)

Numbness feels safe, but it's a con artist. It doesn't protect you—it just puts your pain on layaway. And when it comes back? It brings interest.

So yeah, feeling everything at once is overwhelming. But I'll take the mess over the nothingness any day. Because in the end, you can't heal what you refuse to feel.

Final Thought: You're Not Broken—You're Defrosting

(Let that thaw be awkward. Let it be slow.)

For years, I believed numbness was my edge. My shield. My emotional Teflon. But the truth is, it was just a really convincing illusion. Feeling again is terrifying. But it's also how you come back to life. And the fact that you're reading this—the fact that you're even *thinking* about reconnecting with yourself—is proof that your body is ready. It's terrifying. It's messy. It's uncomfortable. But it's also worth it.

Because in the end, feeling is what makes you alive. And I don't know about you, but I'd rather live in the chaos than stay numb forever.

Learning to Feel Without Losing It

Because emotional numbness isn't a flaw—it's a survival strategy with a damn good résumé.

If you're here, chances are you've spent years toggling between "I feel nothing" and "I feel *everything* and might spontaneously combust." You've mastered the art of keeping it together. But now—maybe for the first time—you're wondering: *What happens if I actually let myself feel?* That question alone is a breakthrough. Don't rush the rest. Start here.

1. Feel Without Forcing

Ask yourself: *What am I feeling right now?*

If your brain throws up a blank screen or shrugs with "nothing," that's not failure. That's data. Shift the question: *What does my body feel like?*

Tight shoulders? Pressure in your chest? Numb legs? That's emotion—in physical form. You're not disconnected. You're translating.

2. Name a Part, Not the Whole

You don't have to find the *perfect* word for what's going on. You don't even have to understand it. Just start here:

"There's a part of me that feels frozen."

"There's a part of me that's afraid to feel."

"There's a part of me that's tired of pretending not to care."

Naming a part gives you breathing room. You're observing—not becoming.

3. Pick One Grounding Sensation Per Day

Small wins. Gentle resets. Five seconds of real-time safety.

30

Place your hand on your chest and feel your heartbeat.
Lie flat on the floor and let gravity remind you: *You're here.*
Run warm water over your hands and just stay there.
This isn't fluffy. It's nervous system repair in real time.

> **Reminder:**
> You don't have to feel everything to heal.
> Feeling *something*—even if it's confusion—is enough.
> Even "I don't know how to do this" is a feeling. And it counts.

Next Up: Who the Hell Am I, Actually?

(Because feeling isn't the finish line—it's the beginning)

So, you've started to feel again. The numbness is cracking. The static's fading. You're feeling… things. (Hooray? Panic? Both?) But now that you've defrosted, a new kind of crisis shows up: *If I'm not just the person who shuts down, powers through, or ghosts their own emotions—then who the hell am I?*

Before we dive back into fear responses and coping chaos, let's take a breather. A self-discovery pit stop. Because healing gets a lot less confusing when you know what emotional animal you're working with.

Who the Hell Am I, Actually?

How to Finally Stop Guessing and Let a Quiz Drag You Instead

(Because you can't fix what you haven't named—and denial isn't a personality type)

You've thawed out a little. You're no longer floating through life entirely numb—congrats. Now you're just mildly confused, existentially disoriented, and wondering what it means to feel again without combusting. You're realizing, *"Wait... if I'm not the emotionless shell who powers through everything, then who the hell am I?"*

Before we dive headfirst into the emotional demolition derby that is fear, survival responses, and your over-functioning nervous system, let's pause. This is your self-awareness pit stop. A low-effort, high-insight vibe check to help you figure out what kind of emotional animal you actually are. Because healing isn't just about feeling your feelings—it's about understanding *who's feeling them.*

Why This Actually Matters

Self-discovery: less BuzzFeed quiz, more emotional survival toolkit.

I know, I know—personality tests get a bad rap. But hear me out: healing gets *infinitely* easier when you stop winging it and start naming your patterns. When you can say, "Ohhh, this is my Enneagram 6 paranoia talking," instead of spiraling into a full identity crisis and blaming your zodiac sign, you

32

reclaim power.

These quizzes won't fix you (spoiler: you're not broken), but they will help you decode the mess—your wiring, your coping strategies, your relationship habits, and all the weird emotional gymnastics you inherited, improvised, or downloaded under duress.

You don't need to take every test. Just pick one—or three, if you're an anxious achiever who likes to over-prepare for hypothetical emotional exams.

You might laugh. You might cry. You'll *definitely* feel called out. Good. That means it's working.

Step 1: Take One (or More) of These Tests and Prepare to Be Lovingly Roasted

(Self-awareness sometimes comes with a side of existential slapstick.)

Enneagram: The One That Tells You Why You're a Walking Coping Mechanism

Ah yes, the Enneagram. The test that doesn't just describe you—it snitches on your trauma response. It explains why you over-function, emotionally ghost, or become suspicious of anyone who texts back too fast.

I got Type 5: The Investigator. I'll give you a second to recover from the shocking revelation that your solitude-craving, boundary-enforcing, deep-diving author is *indeed* an emotional raccoon who hoards data instead of feelings.

What That Means for Me:

I'm fiercely independent to the point of isolation. If I agree to plans, I'm secretly praying you cancel. I'll disappear into a six-hour research rabbit hole just to understand why I overanalyze relationships, and yes, I process emotions like a cat watching a thunderstorm—from a distance, with mild contempt. Vulnerability? Love it in theory. In practice? Pass.

Take the test: personalitypath.com

33

VIA Character Strengths: The One That Gasses You Up—Then Gently Wrecks You

Unlike the Enneagram, which kicks down your emotional door with a clipboard, the VIA test rolls in with a compliment and a side-eye. It tells you your strengths—then quietly shows you which ones took a smoke break during your last spiral.

My Top Five Strengths:

- **Honesty** – I don't do small talk. I do "deeply inconvenient truth at 2am."
- **Love** – I fiercely protect my inner circle. Everyone else? Proceed with caution.
- **Humor** – Equal parts trauma response and survival skill.
- **Gratitude** – Therapy told me to be grateful. Eventually, I listened.
- **Hope** – Somehow, I still believe people can change. Annoying, right?

Take the test: viacharacter.org

Attachment Style: The One That Explains Why You Panic-Text and Then Ghost

Attachment theory—the ultimate "why am I like this?" explainer. It exposes every sabotaged relationship, every unspoken boundary, and every time you reread a text for "tone" like it holds the secrets of the universe.

My Breakdown:

- **Secure: 33.3%** – Allegedly, I'm emotionally stable. Who knew?
- **Anxious: 19.7%** – That part that refreshes text messages like it's a heartbeat monitor.
- **Avoidant: 25.6%** – The flinch that kicks in when someone gets too close.
- **Disorganized: 21.4%** – A delightful swirl of "Come closer!" and "Ew,

no."

Basically, I function *just enough* to pass for securely attached in daylight, but don't ask me to process anything without five drafts and a snack.

Take the test: traumasolutions.com/attachment-styles-quiz

Big Five: The One That Confirms What You Already Suspected (But With Science)

If you want a no-nonsense psychological breakdown of why you're the way you are, this one's for you. Think Myers-Briggs's emotionally unavailable cousin who works in a lab and drinks black coffee.

My Scores:

- **Openness: 15** – I like reality. I do not enjoy improv.
- **Conscientiousness: 31** – Structured but allergic to micromanagement.
- **Extraversion: 53** – I'm social… in bursts. Then I hibernate.
- **Agreeableness: 46** – Reasonable until you cross me.
- **Neuroticism: 26** – Calm, but always watching.

My Score Code: 37k-29m-51k-51v-32C (Plug into the comparison tool and see who you'd vibe with—or block on sight.)

Take the test: outofservice.com/bigfive

Step 2: Actually Look at Your Results

(Don't take the test and then ghost it like your last emotionally unavailable situationship.)

Let's be honest—you didn't just take these quizzes for fun. You took them because you're searching for language, for clarity, for something that makes your inner chaos make sense.

So don't just screenshot your results and move on. Sit with them. Ask:

- What made me uncomfortable?
- What felt *too* accurate?
- What did I laugh at because it hit way too close?

Patterns matter. These results aren't your identity—they're your instruction manual. And they'll become your secret weapon later when we dive into your triggers, relationships, and that fear voice whispering *"don't get too happy, it won't last."*

Final Thoughts

Self-awareness isn't a cage—it's a compass.

These quizzes won't change your life, but they *will* help you stop gaslighting yourself. You'll learn how you operate. How your brain and body make decisions under pressure. And most importantly, how to stop seeing your survival traits as moral failures.

So now that you've been dragged, flattered, and mildly emotionally rearranged, it's time to take that data and run with it.

Because knowing who you are? That's step one.

Knowing what fear does *with* that information?

That's where the good stuff begins.

Next Up: Fear Is a Liar (But Damn, It's Convincing)

Now that you've taken the quizzes, gotten emotionally humbled by your own brain chemistry, and maybe discovered that your top strength is *"making everything a joke to avoid vulnerability"*—let's talk about the next roadblock: fear.

Because here's the kicker—knowing yourself doesn't mean you suddenly stop sabotaging yourself. You can understand your attachment style, personality wiring, and childhood trauma *and still* find yourself pulling away the second things feel safe. That's not because you're a lost cause. It's because fear doesn't care how self-aware you are. Fear is persuasive. Fear is petty. Fear sounds *reasonable* when it whispers things like: *"You're not ready."* *"You'll ruin this." "Better to stay small than to risk being seen and rejected."*

So before we start unlearning survival mode, we need to get up close and personal with the voice trying to keep you in it. Not because it's evil—but because it's confused. Fear's not trying to destroy you. It's trying to *protect* you—loudly, poorly, and with all the finesse of a toddler holding a taser.

Next, we're naming that fear, exposing its tactics, and dragging it into the daylight where it can't control you anymore. You don't need less fear—you just need to stop letting it drive the bus. Let's go.

Fear Is a Liar (But Damn, It's Convincing)

The Fear Disguised as Productivity

(When panic dresses like progress)

Ever stared at a to-do list so long you start color-coding your procrastination? Or convince yourself you're just being "thorough" while you deep-dive every possible outcome of a decision you're still actively avoiding? Welcome to fear—disguised as hyper-productivity, analysis paralysis, and an unholy addiction to certainty. Fear doesn't always show up screaming. Sometimes it just quietly micromanages your every move. It whispers, "What if you miss a detail?" or, "What if this isn't the right choice?" and of course, "What if you regret it later and it ruins everything forever?"

But fear isn't only disguised as productivity. Sometimes it wears the mask of avoidance. It's the person who says, "I just need space to think," then vanishes into video games, Netflix loops, and six hours of Instagram reels. Or the one who jokes their way out of real conversations. Fear is a shapeshifter. And it will wear whatever mask keeps you from moving forward.

My Flavor of Fear: The Unknown

(Not knowing isn't just uncomfortable—it's intolerable)

Some people fear failure. Others fear rejection. Me? I fear not knowing. Not knowing what's coming, how it will feel, or whether I'll survive the other side of it. Honestly, you could hand me a full itinerary of upcoming pain and I'd choose that over the blank page every time—at least then I know what shoes to wear. Anxiety is my default when things get fuzzy. I don't freeze. I wind up. I go full detective. I over-explain, over-prepare, and overanalyze like my nervous system thinks I'm prepping for emotional combat.

While some people dissociate or retreat, I clean the house. Which, let's be honest, only creates more chaos before it creates order. There's nothing like spiraling while knee-deep in a pile of "things I might need someday." I reread instructions three times. Then Google five more versions. I write and rewrite a text I still won't send, because I haven't found the phrasing that guarantees no one will be upset, confused, or mildly inconvenienced. From the outside, it looks productive. But it's panic in disguise.

My brain doesn't scream *DANGER!*—it just gently insists, "Figure it out before something bad happens." And honestly, that's worse. Because it sounds just reasonable enough to be convincing.

Not Everyone Spins—Some Freeze

(Fear wears both sneakers and cement boots)

Not everyone has my version of fear. Some don't spiral—they go still. They freeze. They stare at the task they know they should be doing—responding to the email, making the phone call, apologizing—and just... can't. Their brain slams the emergency brake. They either go emotionally numb or vanish behind a wall of "I'm fine."

Fear doesn't always make you move. Sometimes, it glues you to the floor.

Why Fear Is So Damn Loud

(And why it's not actually irrational)

Here's the thing: fear isn't ridiculous. It's just overprotective. Your amygdala—the brain's built-in fire alarm—is designed to spot danger and keep you alive. But it doesn't know the difference between a bear charging at you and hitting "send" on a vulnerable email. Your nervous system reads both as a potential death sentence.

Anxiety isn't just fear turned up. It's fear that doesn't trust the pause button. It's fear with a caffeine addiction and a spreadsheet. And when your body doesn't see a clear outcome—or worse, sees *too many*—your brain tries to control all of them at once. That's how fear morphs into anxiety: it stops being a moment of "oh no" and becomes a never-ending loop of "but what if...?"

For some, fear gets loud. For others, it gets quiet. It hides in conflict avoidance, withdrawal, or silence. Not because the person doesn't care—but because their inner voice says, "If you show up, you'll screw it up." That silence is still fear. It just shows up in different clothes.

You're Not Weak. You're Overprotected.

(Fear isn't fragility—it's adaptation)

The fear of the unknown usually isn't about the unknown itself. It's about safety. Control. The desperate need not to be blindsided—especially if life has taught you that unpredictability equals pain.

Underneath my fear are questions that sound logistical but are actually trauma echoes. What if I can't handle it? What if I'm not enough? What if it's just like last time? Those aren't simple worries. They're the residue of lived experience.

And maybe your version of fear is different. Maybe it's not about uncertainty. Maybe you're scared of what people will think if you mess up. Maybe you avoid action, not because you're lazy—but because shame is waiting with a megaphone. It's not that you don't know what to do—it's that the consequences of doing it *wrong* feel unbearable. That's not weakness. That's fear trying to protect you from pain by keeping you small.

My Parts, My Protectors

(Fear doesn't show up alone—it brings friends)

When fear kicks in, my internal team scrambles like a pit crew during a crash. The Researcher wants to find the one book or podcast that will make everything make sense. The Over-Apologizer is already drafting everyone's apology email just in case someone *might* be uncomfortable. The Narrator starts psychoanalyzing me in real-time. The Perfectionist panics: "This better be flawless or people will leave and you'll die. Probably."

These parts don't shut down. They hustle. They think they're helping me avoid disaster by staying ten steps ahead. But all they're really doing is keeping me so busy preparing that I never actually move forward.

Other people have their own fear crew. There's the Shut-Down Protector who says, "Better to say nothing than risk saying the wrong thing." The Hyper-Avoidant Self-Talker who whispers, "I'll deal with it tomorrow," which really means never. And the Smiling Mask who cracks jokes to dodge being seen. Whatever your version looks like, know this: your fear parts aren't broken. They're trying to keep you safe. They're just stuck in roles you've outgrown.

When You Can't Think or Feel Your Way Through It

(You don't need more answers—you need movement)

Here's the hard truth: you can't outthink the unknown. You can't research your way to certainty. You can't plan your way around pain. At some point, you have to move—imperfectly, messily, scared.

Fear doesn't vanish when you're "ready." It goes quiet when you move anyway. That's how you teach your body that uncertainty isn't a death sentence. It's just unfamiliar territory. And if your fear is rooted in shame, you don't soothe it with perfection. You heal it by showing up flawed—and realizing the world didn't end.

The Truth You Already Know (But Need to Hear Again)

(Fear is not the enemy—control is)

Fear isn't bad—it's just loud. And often wrong. And dressed up in strategy. But it's not the voice of truth. It's the voice of survival. Of caution. Of lived experience that doesn't yet know the present is different from the past.

Letting fear lead means staying in the cycle: overthinking, hiding, apologizing, freezing. Letting *Self* lead means stepping into the unknown, even with trembling hands and a shaking voice. Fear says, "You can't handle this." But healing whispers back, "You already have."

Fear Management for Functional Adults

You don't have to conquer it—you just have to stop letting it drive.

You just named the thing most people spend a lifetime dodging: fear. And you didn't flinch. That matters. Now comes the real shift—learning to hear fear without handing it the keys. These aren't power poses or pep talks. They're nervous system strategies for when fear's voice gets too loud to ignore.

1. Let Fear Talk—Without Letting It Drive

Ask: *What is my fear trying to protect me from?*

Then hand it the mic (temporarily):

"If I move forward, I'll regret it."

"If I mess this up, I'll be rejected."

"If I slow down, I'll lose control."

These aren't truths. They're protection scripts. Let fear say its piece—then remind it that you, not panic, are the one driving this bus now.

2. Make a One-Inch Move

What's fear blocking right now? Shrink it.

Draft the email—but don't send it.

Write the idea—but don't pitch it yet.

Say, "I'm scared, but I'm trying."

Fear will scream that small steps don't count. That's a lie. One-inch moves reroute entire patterns.

3. Identify Your Fear Part Without Shaming It

Try this:

"The part of me that panics is trying to _____."

"The part of me that avoids is afraid that _____."

Naming the fear creates space between *you* and *it*. That space is where your choices live.

> **Reminder:**
> Fear doesn't need to disappear before you act.
> You just need to know who's talking—and decide who gets to speak louder.
> Hint: it's you.

Next Up: The Chronic Fight-or-Flight Life

(What happens when survival mode becomes your baseline)

You've met your fear. You've named the parts. You've seen how panic can wear the mask of planning, perfectionism, or total shutdown. But what happens when fear stops being a reaction—and becomes your default? When your body is always on high alert, even in silence? When stillness feels suspicious and safety makes you flinch?

That's not just anxiety. That's your nervous system stuck in survival mode.

Next, we're going to talk about what it means to live in a chronic state of fight-or-flight—and how to gently, slowly teach your body it's finally safe to exhale.

The Chronic Fight-or-Flight Life

When Your Nervous System Thinks You Live in a War Zone

(Because sometimes "fine" feels like a setup)

You ever have one of those days where nothing bad is happening, but your body is acting like you're about to be ambushed in a dark alley? Yeah. Welcome to the chronic fight-or-flight life. Logically, you know you're fine. There's no actual danger. No threat. Just another Tuesday. But your nervous system? It missed the memo. It's still scanning for threats like a conspiracy theorist with a corkboard and red string. For some of us, this isn't just an occasional stress response—it's the default. Waking up already exhausted because your body spent the night prepping for disaster. Reacting to a mildly annoying email like you've been drafted into emotional combat. Struggling to relax because the second you let your guard down, some part of you is convinced something awful is going to happen.

And no, this isn't just "anxiety." This is what it looks like when your nervous system never learned how to stand down.

The Connection Between Trauma, Burnout, and Chronic Exhaustion

(The stress cycle that never hit 'reset')

Your body wasn't built to live in survival mode forever. The fight-flight-freeze-fawn response is supposed to kick in during emergencies—like, *oh no, a bear!* You react. Your body mobilizes. And when the threat's gone, you settle back down. But trauma rewires that sequence. If you grew up in chaos, unpredictability, or chronic stress, your nervous system never got the "all clear." It adapted by staying on guard.

That's how you end up with chronic exhaustion even after ten hours of sleep, because your body doesn't know how to rest. It's how you find yourself unable to fully relax—because if you're not alert, who's watching for danger? You might feel lazy or unmotivated, but really, you're just running on fumes. Your brain has been trained to expect a hidden threat in every interaction. When your baseline is "brace for impact," your body carries the cost.

How to Stop Living Like You're Always Bracing for Impact

(You can't heal what your body still thinks is happening)

Here's the problem: your brain doesn't distinguish between real danger and *perceived* danger. That stressful Zoom meeting? Your body treats it like a predator. So how do you convince your nervous system that the world isn't on fire?

1. Learn to Recognize When You're Activated

Your nervous system doesn't send you a polite heads-up. It sends symptoms. Shoulders tense, jaw clenched, breath shallow, heart racing, mind spiraling over something small? That's activation. Step one is just noticing.

2. Interrupt the Pattern

Once you catch it, disrupt it. Shake out your limbs—yes, really. Animals do this instinctively to release survival energy. Try slow breathing, like

45

you're sneaking back into the house past curfew. Or go cold: splash your face, run icy water over your hands, hold an ice cube. These jolt your system into *now*.

3. Convince Your Body That Rest is Safe

Don't aim for full relaxation. Just try micro-moments. Breathe deeply for five minutes before bed. Lie on the floor and do absolutely nothing for sixty seconds. Whisper to yourself, "I don't have to be on guard right now." Your body won't believe you at first. But repetition rewires belief. Calm stops feeling like a trap and starts feeling like safety.

How Chronic Stress Played Out in My Life

(Spoiler: intuition isn't just panic with a spreadsheet)

I spent years in a permanent state of *What's next?* Not in a hopeful, goal-oriented way—in a "what fresh hell is coming" kind of way. Hypervigilance wasn't a quirk; it was a survival strategy. I could read a room before I walked into it. Predict moods. Adapt fast. People called it intuition. But real intuition is quiet, steady. Mine was a frantic scan for potential landmines.

Even when I was still, my brain was racing. I'd rehearse conversations, anticipate conflict, run a mental to-do list that never shut off. I lived in overdrive until I couldn't anymore. Then I'd collapse—dissociating, numbing, disappearing. Not out of choice, but because I literally couldn't function. And then? I'd start the cycle all over again.

If that sounds familiar, hear this: you're not broken. You're not dramatic. You're not lazy. You're just living in a body that adapted to chaos—and never got the memo that it's safe now.

When Calm Feels Suspicious

(Because your body learned peace is always followed by pain)

Even in the rare moments when nothing was wrong, I still couldn't settle. I'd sit in the quiet, waiting. Because there's *always* a next problem, right? Even joy felt like a setup. I'd think, "This is nice... but how long will it last?" or "Something bad always happens after things go well." So instead of relaxing, I braced.

And that's how the loop continues. You never truly rest, because your body doesn't trust safety. Calm feels like vulnerability. Stillness feels like exposure. Your nervous system learned: if you're not ready, you'll get hurt. And it stayed ready.

Final Thought

*(You're not overreacting. You're over-adapted.)*If you've spent your life scanning for danger, waiting for the next hit, feeling like rest is weakness or peace is suspicious—you're not broken. You're over-adapted. Your body learned to survive in a world that kept you on edge. But you don't have to live there anymore. Your nervous system can relearn safety. You can slowly, gently, unhook from survival mode. You don't have to be on guard forever.

I promise—nothing bad will happen if you let yourself breathe.

Tools for the High-Functioning Wreck

Because scanning the room like a CIA agent isn't your personality—it's your trauma talking.

You've spent years in survival mode. Scanning. Spiraling. Over-functioning like it was your full-time job—and still managing to show up like everything was fine. That's not dysfunction. That's high-functioning trauma. But now that you've named it, your body needs something new: permission to *stand down.* Not forever. Just for today.

1. Do a 10-Second Safety Scan

Sit. Breathe. Ask: *Am I actually in danger... or just rehearsing for it?*

Check your jaw. Your shoulders. Your stomach.

Softening isn't surrender—it's feedback for a nervous system that forgot what calm feels like.

You're not gaslighting your fear. You're offering it new information.

2. Choose a "Safe Enough" Anchor

One thing. One sense. One moment.

A warm drink. Lying flat on the floor. Running your fingers across something textured.

No multitasking. No fixing. Just feel it.

Let your body register: *This moment is not a threat.*

3. Practice Micro-Rest Without Guilt

Forget the two-hour nap. If stillness feels unsafe, try sixty seconds.

Set a one-minute timer. Breathe. Say:

"This minute is mine. I don't have to earn it."

Then move on. That's it. That counts.

> **Reminder:**
> You don't have to break down to slow down.
> You don't need to collapse to rest.
> Regulating before you crash isn't indulgence.
> It's how you reclaim your life.

Next Up: Ten Years, One Wrong Diagnosis, and a Whole Lot of WTF

(When your trauma gets mislabeled—and you get lost in the process)

Now that you know your nervous system wasn't overreacting—it was over-functioning—let's talk about what happens when the world doesn't see that. When your trauma responses are mistaken for character flaws. When people look at your survival skills and call them pathology.

Next, we're diving into the decade I spent under the wrong diagnosis. Because when your pain is misunderstood, you don't just waste time—you lose trust in yourself.

Let's talk about misdiagnosis, emotional whiplash, and what it means to finally call your experience by its real name.

Ten Years, One Wrong Diagnosis, and a Whole Lot of WTF

Putting My Pain in the Wrong File

(When the label doesn't match the wound)

I didn't always know I had trauma. That's the wild part. You can live through emotional chaos, operate with a nervous system permanently on fire, and still believe the real issue is... you. For years, I thought I was defective. Like everyone else had a user manual for life, and I was out here trying to hotwire a broken system with a frayed cord and blind optimism.

So when I got diagnosed with Borderline Personality Disorder (BPD) in my early twenties, it actually felt like relief. A name. A box. A reason I felt like a walking red flag. My relationships were wreckage. My emotions were loud. My fear of abandonment deserved an Olympic medal. And in true overachiever fashion, I set out to fix it. I did DBT—not once, but twice. I meditated, journaled, filled out every worksheet like it was an emotional SAT prep course. And it helped... on the surface. I could regulate. I could pause. I could explain my triggers like a trauma-informed TED Talk.

But underneath all that awareness, I still felt like I was bracing for something bad to happen. Like I could never fully exhale. I had mastered the language of healing, but I still didn't feel safe in my own skin. And the question that haunted me quietly, consistently, kept rising:

Why does my nervous system still feel like it's on fire when I've done everything

49

right?

Spoiler Alert: It Wasn't BPD

(And no, that wasn't obvious at the time)

Here's what no one tells you: when you're a woman with big feelings and messy relationships, the default diagnosis is often BPD. Especially in the early 2010s, when C-PTSD wasn't even on the clinical radar. Trauma was still reserved for war zones and car crashes—not for childhood neglect, emotional chaos, or growing up in a home where safety was conditional and love had strings attached.

So I accepted the diagnosis. I wore it like a scarlet letter. But eventually, something didn't sit right. As much as the BPD label helped explain certain patterns, it missed the rest. It didn't explain the detachment. The numbness. The addiction. The whiplash of feeling everything, then nothing at all. I wasn't just reactive. I was dissociating. I wasn't just impulsive. I was surviving.

2022: The Year I Stopped Fixing the Wrong Problem

(Rock bottom, then lower—and finally, clarity)

I was first diagnosed in 2012, right after my gastric bypass surgery. That season cracked everything open. The food coping was gone, but the pain was still there—unprocessed, unrelenting. My kids were born in 2007 and 2009—bright, beautiful constants in a life unraveling at the seams. I loved them fiercely, but by 2015, I had nothing left. Alcohol became my escape. Then drugs. By 2016, I was spiraling—and eventually ended up on probation.

In one of the hardest decisions I've ever made, I signed over guardianship of my children to my parents. Not because I didn't love them, but because I knew I couldn't keep them safe while I was barely functioning. I lost custody, but I never stopped being their mom. I just stopped being the one raising them.

Then came a period of sobriety—from 2016 to 2020, I pulled myself together. I was stable. But healing? Not so much. 2020 brought a divorce. A move across the country. And by January 2021, I was back in the Midwest—not to start over, but to survive.

Ten years. So many rock bottoms I stopped counting and started calling it "the basement."

Then in 2022, a therapist handed me *The Body Keeps the Score*. And just like that, it all clicked. Everything I had been trying to fix—every emotional loop, every "flaw," every shutdown—wasn't BPD.

It was C-PTSD.

And that changed everything.

C-PTSD vs. BPD: Same Behaviors, Different Story

(This isn't semantics—it's survival)

Let's be clear: C-PTSD and BPD can look alarmingly similar. Emotional dysregulation. Identity confusion. Fear of abandonment. Rollercoaster relationships. But here's the crucial difference—BPD is a personality disorder. C-PTSD is a trauma response.

One says, *This is who you are.*

The other says, *This is what happened to you.*

That distinction isn't just clinical. It's existential. Because when I finally realized I was dealing with trauma, not a broken personality, the narrative shifted. I wasn't too much. I was conditioned. I wasn't unstable. I was unprotected.

The Damage of Being Misdiagnosed

(It's not just the wrong treatment—it's the wrong story)

Being misdiagnosed didn't just waste time. It warped my self-concept. I believed I was inherently flawed. That my emotional intensity was a defect, not a history. That I was unlovable. Overwhelming. Hard to be around.

But the diagnosis wasn't the whole problem—it was the lack of context.

Because when you slap a label on someone without asking *what happened to them*, you're not just diagnosing. You're branding. And that kind of framing makes healing feel impossible.

When you believe your pain *is* your personality, how do you separate who you are from what you've been through?

The Shift: From Broken to Conditioned

(And finally, a roadmap that made sense)

When I understood it was C-PTSD, something shifted. I stopped trying to fix myself. I started trying to *retrain* myself. My nervous system didn't need judgment—it needed safety. I wasn't reacting because I was irrational. I was reacting because my brain had been taught that love was volatile, stability was temporary, and peace was suspicious.

The goal wasn't perfection. The goal was safety.

Not just for my body—but for my internal parts, too.

Final Thought: Your Diagnosis Isn't Your Identity

(Even if it felt like one)

If you've ever been misdiagnosed—if someone handed you a label that didn't quite fit and you wore it anyway out of desperation to understand yourself—please hear this: You are not your diagnosis. You are not your trauma responses. You are not hard to love.

You were surviving without a map. And now?

Now you get to learn how to live.

Untangling the Lie

When the diagnosis didn't fit—but the damage still stuck.

Being misunderstood isn't just frustrating—it's disorienting. A misdiagnosis doesn't just change your treatment plan. It rewrites your identity in someone else's handwriting. If you're here, you've probably been living with the side effects of someone else's story about you. Let's start writing a truer one.

1. Reclaim Your Narrative (Gently)

Complete this sentence:

"They told me I was _____, but what I really needed was _____."

Don't edit. Don't intellectualize. Let the truth spill out the way it always wanted to. That line alone can unravel years of silence.

2. Make a List of Survival, Not Symptoms

Write down 3–5 traits you've been told were problems.

Then translate them through the lens of survival:

- *"Too sensitive"* → *Scanned for danger early.*
- *"Too reactive"* → *Learned to adapt fast in unpredictable spaces.*
- *"Detached"* → *Protected yourself from emotional collapse.*

These weren't character flaws. They were brilliant adaptations. You didn't malfunction—you adapted.

3. Create a "What Actually Helped" List

Forget what was prescribed. What *worked*?

The book that hit like truth.

The person who saw you without flinching.

The moment your body finally exhaled.

Write it down. That's your medicine. Your map. Your evidence that healing never needed to come with a label.

> **Reminder:**
> Your pain is not a personality disorder.
> You are not too much, too broken, or too late.
> You weren't the problem.

53

You were surviving a story that never fit—and now you're rewriting it.

Next Up: The Shit You Took Personally That Wasn't Yours

(Because carrying other people's dysfunction is a full-time job you didn't apply for)

Maybe the diagnosis didn't fit. Maybe the labels they gave you said more about *them* than you. But here's the thing: when you're misunderstood long enough, you start turning that confusion inward. You start believing you're the problem. That your reactions were wrong. That your pain was too loud.

Next, we're talking about the shame you absorbed, the projections you mistook for truth, and the emotional weight that was *never* yours to carry in the first place.

The Shit You Took Personally That Wasn't Yours

Did You Know? Shame Can Motivate People to Do Just About Anything—Except Heal

(Because nothing screams "growth" like blaming yourself for everything)

Shame is sneaky. It keeps people quiet when they need to speak. Small when they should take up space. It convinces them that every failed relationship, awkward moment, and 2AM mental replay session is solid proof that *they* are the problem. If you've ever found yourself reliving a three-year-old conversation and whispering, *"Yep, that's probably when everyone started hating me,"* congrats. You've been personally victimized by your own brain.

And if love, safety, or acceptance felt conditional growing up? Your nervous system probably auto-installed a default setting: *If something goes wrong, I must've caused it.* You weren't taught healthy accountability. You were handed an all-inclusive, auto-renewing self-blame package—complete with lifetime access to **Why Am I Like This**™. And just like that, shame made *you* the problem.

The Shame Spiral: Why You Keep Blaming Yourself for Things That Weren't Your Fault

(AKA: That one mental teacup ride you can't get off of)

Shame doesn't always announce itself. Sometimes it starts small—you mess up, overshare, say something a little too honest. No big deal, right? Wrong. Your brain, ever the overachiever, immediately opens a folder labeled *Evidence of Suckage* and pulls out every moment from fifth grade to last Tuesday. That email you regret. That smile you now swear was fake. That joke no one laughed at.

Suddenly, you're not just someone who made a mistake. You *are* the mistake. And you don't even realize the original moment wasn't that serious. You're carrying a history of shame messages that taught you to default to *It must be me.* Your nervous system's been running that script since childhood.

How You Were Taught You're Either Too Much or Not Enough

(Spoiler: You were neither)

You don't just wake up with trust issues and a nervous system that treats minor conflict like a full-scale betrayal. You learned that from the people who were supposed to teach you safety. If your childhood sounded like, *"Stop being so dramatic,"* or *"That never happened—you're remembering it wrong,"* then your body internalized a dangerous rule: *Blame yourself first.*

Maybe you were labeled *too much*—too emotional, too reactive, too needy. So you shrank. You stuffed your voice into silence until it became muscle tension and vague dread. Or maybe you were made to feel *not enough*—not lovable, not stable, not worth softness. So you hustled. You worked harder, tried to earn love like it was a performance review.

And none of it worked. Because the problem wasn't you. It was the dysfunction you were forced to absorb.

56

When You Go from Victim to Villain (Because You Set a Boundary)

New role unlocked: "Too Much" with a side of "Unreasonable"

There's a particular kind of gaslighting that happens when you stop apologizing for being mistreated. The moment you set a boundary, stop catering to chaos, or say *no* for the first time in years? Suddenly you're not the "hurt one"—you're the *problem*. You're cold. Difficult. Not who you used to be. And the same people who ignored your pain will resent your healing. Why? Because your growth disrupts the story where *they* were always the good guy.

You went from being someone they "worried about" to someone they warn others about. Not because you became cruel. But because you stopped carrying their emotional mess. And they hate that.

Here's the truth: People who benefitted from your self-abandonment will always call your boundaries betrayal. Let them. You're not here to be understood by people committed to misunderstanding you. You're not here to keep the peace at the cost of your sanity. You were never the villain. You were just done being collateral damage.

You Don't Need to "Fix" Yourself—Just Change the Story

(Because self-blame only ever gave you the illusion of control)

You might be thinking, *Okay, so I'm not broken—just molded by shame like emotional Play-Doh.* Great. Now what? Well, the "fixing yourself" narrative? Let's burn it. You don't need to be fixed. You need to rewire a story that was never yours to carry.

Self-blame used to be your power play. If everything was your fault, maybe you could control it. Be better. Be easier. Be enough. But now? You're not the same scared kid trying to earn love with perfection. You get to ask—*Do I still want to believe that?* Because spoiler: **You don't have to.**

57

Final Thought: You Were Never the Problem

(But the shame sure was)

If you take one thing from this chapter, let it be this:

You weren't too emotional.

You weren't too much.

You weren't broken.

You were asking for safety in a world that didn't know how to give it.

That's not a flaw. That's a survival instinct.

And now that you see it? You get to choose something different. You don't have to shrink. You don't have to hustle for worth. And you definitely don't have to carry other people's failures like they belong to you.

Shame Disruption Kit

Because shame's favorite trick is convincing you it's just telling the truth.

Shame doesn't shout—it whispers. It rewrites your story in second-person self-loathing: *You're too much. You're a burden. You'll always mess this up.* And worst of all? It sounds familiar. Here's how to take the pen back—one sentence, one interruption, one truth at a time.

1. Call It Out: "This Is Shame Talking"

That voice in your head saying, *"I ruin everything"* or *"No one actually likes me"?* Yeah—that's not insight. That's shame, dressed in your voice, trying to pass as fact.

Pause. Say it out loud: *"This is shame talking. Not truth."*

You are not the voice. You're the one hearing it—and now, questioning it.

2. Reclaim Your Role in the Story

Complete this:

"I was made to believe I was _____, but I was actually _____."

Example: *"I was made to believe I was too emotional, but I was actually emotionally attuned."*

58

These aren't Pinterest affirmations. These are counter-narratives. These are *corrections.*

3. Create a Shame-Escape Plan

The 2AM spiral will come. Don't pretend it won't. Prepare for it instead. Build a kit:

- A grounding phrase like *"This moment isn't the whole story."*
- A photo or name of someone who sees the real you.
- A sensory anchor: cold water, soft texture, a scent that calms, or a playlist that pulls you back to center.

You don't have to "defeat" shame. You just need to interrupt the loop.

Reminder:
You are not too much. You are not broken.
You were never meant to carry what they handed you.
Drop it. Walk away. Reclaim your voice.

Next Up: When Your Trauma Makes You the Problem

(Because healing doesn't always look graceful from the outside)

So maybe the shame isn't yours. Maybe the weight you carried was never yours to begin with. But just as you start feeling lighter, someone tells you you've changed. That you're harder to be around. That you're not who you used to be. And suddenly, the self-blame creeps back in.

Let's talk about what happens when your survival strategies get mislabeled as character flaws—and how to stop apologizing for the ways you kept yourself alive.

When Your Trauma Makes You the Problem

How Survival Mode Gets Mistaken for a Personality Disorder

(Because apparently protecting yourself is the real problem now)

Let's start with something no one wants to say out loud:

You didn't choose your trauma. But you did adapt to survive it. And now those adaptations? People treat them like personality defects.

Welcome to the double bind of trauma: You got hurt, so you protected yourself. And now you're "the problem" for having needed protection in the first place. Fun.

"You're So Defensive"

(Translation: You flinched after years of emotional ambushes, and now you're inconvenient)

Ah yes, the fan favorite. The phrase people love to toss out when you dare react to something after a lifetime of being emotionally blindsided.

Defensiveness isn't dysfunction. It's protection. It's your nervous system whispering, *"We've seen this before. It didn't end well."* But instead of curiosity, people meet your defenses with criticism. They don't ask, *"What made you feel unsafe?"* They ask, *"Why are you overreacting?"*

And just like that, your pain gets pathologized. You're not seen as someone with a story—you're labeled as a problem to manage. This is how trauma survivors end up quietly carrying more than anyone knows... while being told they're "too much."

The "Flaws" That Were Just Survival Tactics

Let's play a game: Trauma or Trait?

- **Hyper-independence**
  Trauma says: *No one's coming. I'll do it all myself.*
  The world says: *You're cold. Emotionally unavailable.*
- **People-pleasing**
  Trauma says: *If I keep people happy, I stay safe.*
  The world says: *You're fake. Spineless.*
- **Perfectionism**
  Trauma says: *If I do everything right, no one can hurt me.*
  The world says: *You're obsessive. Controlling.*
- **Emotional numbness**
  Trauma says: *Feeling is dangerous. Stay frozen.*
  The world says: *You're disconnected. Apathetic.*

Let's be clear: these aren't character defects.

They're functional, trauma-born strategies that kept you alive when safety wasn't an option. And you know what? They probably worked. Until they didn't.

Why It Still Feels Like It's Your Fault

(*Because no one taught you how to translate your pain into a language the world respects*)

The people around you didn't learn how to look beyond behavior. They judged how you showed up instead of asking what shaped you. They didn't recognize silence as dissociation—they called it rude. They didn't see outbursts as pain—they called it instability. They didn't understand freeze responses—they called it laziness.

So you twisted yourself smaller. Quieter. Easier to tolerate. Hoping that would finally make the pain stop.

It didn't.

Shame Is the Weapon. Adaptation Is the Wound.

(And most people only ever see the bleeding edge)

Shame doesn't ask *"What happened to you?"* It whispers *"What's wrong with you?"*—quietly, persistently, and always at the worst possible moment. It doesn't care about your story. It skips context and goes straight for character assassination. Over time, it turns coping mechanisms into personality flaws. It takes the ways you protected yourself and repackages them as pathology. And just like that, your entire emotional blueprint gets rewritten with defectiveness as the headline.

But here's what's actually true: You weren't "too sensitive"—you just learned to scan for danger early. You weren't "attention-seeking"—you were starved for connection and doing your best to feel seen. You weren't "dramatic"—you were never taught how to express safely, so it came out sideways. You weren't broken. You were backed into a corner and did what you had to do to survive.

You Don't Have to Apologize for How You Survived

(Spoiler: Your humanity isn't a flaw)

I know the inner monologue: *But I do cause problems sometimes...*

Sure. Because you're human.

But there's a difference between shame and accountability.

- **Shame says**: You're fundamentally unworthy.
- **Accountability says**: Now that I understand better, I'll do better.

62

You weren't the problem. You were the result of a system that made survival your only option. And now? You're choosing something more—not because you were wrong, but because you're ready for more than just surviving.

Let's Talk About the Real Problem

(Hint: It's not your freeze response—it's the world's refusal to slow down)

The real issue was never your adaptation.

It's that most people don't speak trauma's language.

So when you flinch, freeze, fawn, spiral, dissociate, or check out—they don't see effort.

They see difficulty.

But what they're really witnessing is *work.*

- The effort to regulate.
- The effort to connect.
- The effort to just. feel. safe.

Maybe your reaction wasn't "too much."

Maybe the expectation that you stay calm while drowning was the real problem.

How to Stop Calling Survival a Character Defect

You don't have to rebuild your whole identity. Just shift the lens—and tell the truth.

What you've been calling "flaws" might just be survival in disguise. Traits you were taught to hate in yourself are often the exact things that kept you afloat. This isn't about excusing everything—it's about understanding where it came from so you can decide what you want to carry forward.

1. Rename the Pattern

Shame says: *You're cold.*

63

Truth says: *You're protecting yourself.*

Shame says: *You're controlling.*

Truth says: *You learned to anticipate everything so nothing could blindside you.*

Call it what it is: a strategy, not a personality flaw.

2. Map the Origin

Ask yourself: *When did I first need this to survive?*

Not in an overthinking way. Just a moment of clarity.

When you locate the why, the shame starts to loosen its grip.

3. Separate Self from Strategy

You aren't the shutdown. You aren't the over-apologizing. You aren't the rage burst.

You used those behaviors.

And if you used them, you can unlearn them. That's power—not pathology.

4. Practice Internal Validation

What would you say to a kid who had to use these same coping tools just to make it through the day?

Now say it to yourself. Like, out loud. Yes, even if it feels weird.

Say it again tomorrow. And the next day. Every damn day—until it stops feeling like a lie.

> **Reminder:**
> You are not your worst moment.
> You are not a broken version of who you *should* be.
> You are the sum of everything you did to survive—and the story you get to rewrite now.

Final Thought: The Problem Was Never You

(Rewriting the Story They Gave You)

You were never too much—you were simply in too much, with no one safe enough to help you hold it. What looked like instability wasn't a flaw; it was your nervous system surviving instability. You weren't broken. You were brilliant—adapting to what your environment demanded without ever being taught another way. And now? Now you get to drop the shame that never belonged to you, carry forward the wisdom you earned, and finally come home to yourself.

Next Up: Burn It All Down

So you've spent years being blamed for the very things that kept you alive. You've mistaken your survival strategies for flaws. You've contorted yourself into something more "palatable," hoping it would finally hurt less.

But now? Now you know better. And once that truth lands—once you realize you were never the problem—something shifts. You start questioning everything you built on top of pain. The life, the identity, the roles you played just to stay safe? Suddenly, none of it fits anymore. And that urge you feel? To disappear. To torch it all. To start fresh? That's not selfish. That's the part of you that's done surviving—and ready to live.

Let's talk about what it really means to burn it down without burning yourself in the process.

Burn It All Down

The Fantasy of Starting Over

(The seductive lie that escape equals freedom)

Ah, the sweet, intoxicating fantasy of torching your entire life and emerging from the ashes as a brand-new, fully optimized human being. No baggage. No past mistakes. Just a crisp, shiny version of you, freshly baked and chaos-free, finally ready to live your best life. Sounds amazing, right?

Too bad it's complete bullshit.

The Urge to Start Over

And why it's just avoidance in disguise

If you've ever fantasized about packing a single suitcase, changing your name, and ghosting every person who ever knew you—congrats, you're not broken. You're just deeply human. When life feels unbearable, the idea of a fresh start is almost erotic. It's why people suddenly move across the country, quit their jobs with flair, or dramatically announce, "This time, I'm finally becoming a whole new person." And sure, sometimes those choices *do* help. Shifting your environment, cutting off toxic relationships, or making bold changes can absolutely be a catalyst for healing.

But let's not confuse bravery with avoidance. There's a difference between leaving a bad situation and running from yourself. And here's the kicker:

66

you can move to a new city, start a new job, block every ex and childhood frenemy, but if you haven't done the inner work, all you're doing is relocating your dysfunction to a prettier backdrop. Trust me—those patterns? They travel light.

Why You Can't Outrun Your Patterns

(Spoiler: your brain comes with you)

Believe me, I tried. I thought if I just changed the scenery, the emotional avalanche would stop. That maybe I wasn't emotionally unavailable—I just needed the right relationship. That my stress wasn't trauma—it was just this job, this version of me, this zip code. I genuinely believed that if I switched up my surroundings, I'd finally feel better.

Spoiler alert: it was me.

If that hits a little too close to home, take a breath. Here's the truth bomb no one likes to unwrap: if the same stories keep playing out in your life— same pain, different people—then the common denominator isn't the city or the circumstances. It's the unhealed parts of you, still trying to write the next chapter with the same broken pen.

The Fantasy of Reinvention (And Why It's a Lie)

(Erasure sounds sexy, but healing's the real glow-up)

Reinvention has incredible branding. It's all new beginnings and blank slates, promising that if you just become someone *better*, you'll never have to sit with regret, shame, or that pit of grief again. I bought in hard. I told myself that if I moved, my problems wouldn't follow. That if I cut people off, I'd finally be free. That if I changed careers, I'd feel fulfilled. That if I completely overhauled my personality, maybe—just maybe—I'd finally be lovable.

Here's what actually happened: I moved and discovered my trauma fit neatly in a carry-on. I ghosted people, but my inner wounds still showed up uninvited. I changed jobs, but burnout followed like a loyal puppy. And that new personality? It was exhausting. Every time I thought a new start would be the answer, my unresolved pain just popped up like, "Oh hey. Still here. Miss me?"

IFS Connection: The Part of You That Thinks Running = Safety

(Your protector isn't the problem—your pain is)

This is where Internal Family Systems (IFS) comes in clutch. IFS teaches us that we're made of inner parts—little versions of ourselves that were shaped by past experiences. And the part of you that wants to run? That's not sabotage. That's a protector. One doing its damn best to keep you safe.

This part believes that if you start over, you'll finally be okay. If you erase the past, it can't hurt you anymore. It's not reckless; it's scared. It remembers what happened last time you stayed too long, trusted too much, or spoke too soon. Running makes sense when pain feels inescapable.

But healing isn't about pretending the past didn't happen. It's about integrating the parts of you that *survived* it, so they're not the ones driving the getaway car every time your nervous system smells a threat.

Burn It Down... But Keep What Matters

(Knowing when to walk away versus when you're just ghosting yourself)

Let's be clear: sometimes walking away *is* the healthiest choice. There's nothing noble about staying in environments that gut your spirit. If something is toxic, abusive, or soul-depleting, leave. Burn that bridge, pack your boundaries, and peace out.

But don't confuse leaving with healing. Burning bridges isn't the same as setting boundaries. Reinvention isn't the same as integration. Before you walk into your next chapter, ask yourself the hard question: am I actually changing, or am I just dragging the same pain into a new setting and hoping the lighting is better?

Because real transformation doesn't come from escape. It comes from turning toward the parts of you you've spent a lifetime trying to outrun—and choosing to stay.

Final Thought: The Only Way Out Is Through

(You don't need a reset. You need a reunion.)

You don't have to erase your past to heal. You don't need to reinvent yourself into someone entirely new just to be worthy of peace. What you *do* need is to stop running long enough to realize that the survival strategies that got you here—those automatic responses, defenses, and coping mechanisms—don't have to keep running the show. You can acknowledge them, thank them for doing their job, and then gently invite them to take a back seat. Healing isn't about becoming someone else; it's about becoming whole. And that starts the moment you stop trying to outrun yourself. That's when real freedom begins.

Tools for When You're Tempted to Torch It All

For when you're halfway through a reinvention spiral but low-key know better.

Here's where things get real. Because insight is cute, but action? That's hotter. Reinvention doesn't start with a vision board—it usually starts with the urge to run. Before you ghost your job, your relationship, or your entire social life, pause and ask the question that changes everything:

"Am I running toward something... or just away from pain?"

If the answer is pain, that's not failure. That's information. You don't have to stay where you are—but you do need to know *why* you're leaving. Because escaping pain without understanding it just guarantees you'll meet it again... in a different outfit, with the same damn storyline.

Next: track the pattern, not just the problem.

If you keep ending up in the same arguments, the same dead-end jobs, the same emotional burnout—*spoiler:* it's not just bad luck. That's a trauma loop. Ask:

69

- *What's the theme here?*
- *What role do I keep playing?*
- *What am I avoiding by changing the scenery instead of the script?*

Still tempted to start fresh? Cool. Then define what *starting over* actually means to you. Reinvention doesn't require amnesia—it requires *integration*. Write this out:

- *What parts of me feel true no matter where I go?*
- *What pain am I dragging behind me like emotional carry-on luggage?*
- *What have I learned—and what do I want to actually keep this time?*

And don't forget the part of you that wants to run. Seriously. Don't exile it. Don't shame it. Don't slap a "self-sabotage" sticker on its forehead. Ask it:

- *What are you afraid will happen if I stay?*
- *What are you hoping we'll avoid by starting over?*

That part isn't reckless. It's protective. It's been trying to save you the only way it knows how. The goal isn't to silence it—it's to lead it somewhere safer.

> **Reminder:**
> You don't need to erase your story to write a new chapter.
> You just need to stop letting the most wounded part of you hold the pen.

Next Up: Part 2 – The Toolbox

(Where insight becomes action)

So you've faced the wreckage. You've named your patterns. You've resisted the seductive siren song of reinvention for reinvention's sake. And now?

Now we do something with all that insight.

Because let's be honest—understanding your trauma isn't the same as healing it. This next part isn't just another "journal your feelings" motivational poster. It's practical. Tactical. Designed for real life, not just Pinterest boards.

You'll learn how to calm your nervous system when it's spiking, talk to your inner parts without freaking them out, and build habits that don't require monk-level consistency. No fluff. No guilt trips. Just real tools for real people who are a little tired, a little jaded, and more than ready to feel okay again.

Let's get to work.

II

Part 2: The Toolbox

Insight is great, but tools are better. This section gives you no-fluff strategies to calm your nervous system, work with your inner parts, and stop spiraling every time life gets loud. You don't need to heal perfectly—you just need a plan.

TOOLKIT: Teaching Your Body You're Safe

No amount of self-reflection will stick if you're in survival mode

Read that again. Because the epiphany won't land if your body is still bracing for impact. I know what you're looking for—the breakthrough. The emotional mic drop. The moment you finally understand why you self-sabotage, why you freeze during conflict, or why your brain replays every awkward conversation from the last ten years on loop. You want the code cracked, the puzzle solved, the closure achieved. And listen, same. But here's the thing no one wants to say out loud:

You can't out-think your biology.

You can't journal your way out of trauma. You can't logic your way into feeling safe. Because healing doesn't start in your thoughts. It starts in your body.

Your Nervous System Runs the Show (And It's Kind of a Jerk About It)

Let's do a vibe check. You logically know something isn't that serious, but your heart is racing like you're being hunted. Someone offers light feedback and your stomach drops like you're thirteen again and just got called into the principal's office. You try to rest, but your body says, "We must stay vigilant! Danger is emotional and invisible but definitely out there!"

Congratulations: you're in survival mode.

75

Your autonomic nervous system has one job—detect threat and keep you alive. It doesn't care how self-aware you are. It doesn't care that your therapist said you're making progress. It doesn't care that the email wasn't *actually* rude. It sees a flicker of danger and slams the panic button like it's collecting commission. This is why you can *know* you're safe and still feel like everything is falling apart.

Stop Running on Monster Energy and Trauma Responses

Before we talk tools, let's set the tone: this is not about faking calm while your insides are screaming. It's not about gaslighting yourself into pretending you're fine for the sake of "positive vibes." And it's definitely not about overriding your body's signals with Pinterest mantras and deep inhales.

We're here to teach your nervous system that it doesn't have to live like you're still under siege. Because as long as your body believes you're in danger, your brain will keep reacting like you are.

Real-Life Regulation Tools

Now that we've set the stage, let's get into the actual tools. These aren't abstract ideas or Pinterest quotes. These are real-life, body-based techniques you can use when your nervous system is in full-blown threat mode. No vibe checks necessary—just practical steps that actually help. Use them when your heart's racing, your brain is spiraling, or your body feels like a live wire.

1. Orienting: Look Around and Name What's Real
Also known as the 5-4-3-2-1 grounding technique

- 5 things you can see
- 4 things you can touch
- 3 things you can hear

- 2 things you can smell
- 1 thing you can taste

Why it works: Your brain can't fully spiral into trauma and engage with the present moment at the same time. This interrupts the panic loop by anchoring you in what's real, right now. (The first time I did this, I got distracted counting dog hairs on my couch. Grounded? Yes. Emotionally thrilled? Absolutely not.)

2. The Ice Trick: Your Nervous System's Reset Button

- Hold an ice cube
- Splash cold water on your face
- Take a cold shower if things feel extreme

Why it works: Cold triggers the parasympathetic nervous system—your internal brake pedal. It's a literal "chill out" for your body. (Fair warning: the first time I tried this, I yelped like I was being murdered. My dog was deeply concerned.)

3. Lion's Breath: When Normal Breathing Isn't Cutting It

- Inhale deeply through your nose
- Exhale forcefully through your mouth while sticking out your tongue like a lion
- Repeat 3–5 times

Why it works: This releases built-up tension and disrupts anxiety's grip on your system. Also, it's nearly impossible to stay stressed while making jungle creature faces. (I resisted this forever because I didn't want to look stupid. Then I remembered: my nervous system embarrasses me on the regular, so honestly, who cares.)

IFS Insight: The Part That Resists Feeling Safe

There's a part of me that cannot chill. I call her The Hypervigilant One. She's always on alert. She watches everyone's tone, notices every micro-expression, and treats rest like a dangerous game. Her core belief? That stillness is risky and safety is an illusion. For a long time, I confused her with my "real self." I thought I was just an anxious person. Turns out, I was listening to a protector who believed that if she stopped scanning for danger, something terrible would happen.

When I stopped shaming that part of me and started hearing her out, things shifted. She still doesn't love meditation, but we're negotiating. She's not wrong for existing. She's just tired—and honestly, I am too.

Check-In: What's Your Nervous System Up To?

So here's your invitation: pause. Tune in. When do you feel most on edge? What kinds of situations make you freeze, shut down, or overreact? What does your body do when it thinks you're under threat—does your chest tighten? Do you feel numb? Do your limbs go heavy, or your mind go blank? And when you *do* try to rest, what thoughts show up uninvited?

Got all that? Great. Now choose one tool. Just one. Try it right now. Because awareness alone won't reset your nervous system. Your body needs evidence—sensory proof—that it's safe again.

Takeaway Truth: Regulation Comes Before Revelation

You can't change your life if your body still thinks it's in danger. That lightbulb moment you've been chasing won't stick if you're still living like you're bracing for the next emotional ambush. Safety isn't just a feeling. It's a physiological state. Teach your body first, and then the breakthroughs will have somewhere to land.

Quick & Dirty Cheat Sheet

If your brain is mush and your body's on high alert, here's your no-fluff breakdown. These are the essentials for teaching your nervous system that it's safe *before* you try to do the deep work.

Goal:

- Shift out of survival mode so your body and mind can actually make use of all that therapy, journaling, and self-reflection.

What Actually Helps:

- **Grounding** (5-4-3-2-1 method)
- **Cold exposure** (ice cube, cold water, shower)
- **Breathwork** (Lion's Breath or any intentional breathing pattern that slows your system)

Therapy Tie-Ins:

- **DBT:** Grounding, mindfulness, distress tolerance
- **IFS:** Comforting and listening to your hypervigilant parts
- **Nervous System Regulation:** Somatic tools like orienting and cold exposure

Important Reminder:

- You cannot out-think your biology. If your body believes it's under threat, no amount of logic will override it.

Bonus Points:

- Practice *one* regulation tool daily
- Consistency > Perfection

- You're not trying to master it—you're trying to rewire safety into your system through repetition

Coming off survival mode? Beautiful. But just a heads up—now we enter the part of healing where your inner critic wakes up from its nap, rubs its hands together, and starts whispering trash talk into your brain under the guise of "self-improvement." That's what we're tackling next.

You ready? Good. Let's go meet the voice that swears it's helpful but secretly hates your guts.

TOOLKIT: The Inner Critic Isn't the Problem—Shame Is

Because self-compassion works better than self-destruction—who knew?

If the phrase *self-love* makes your eye twitch, you're not alone. It often comes bundled with overpriced green juice, toxic positivity, and the kind of spiritual bypassing that makes you want to throw a crystal through a window. Maybe you've tried positive affirmations and felt like a complete fraud. Maybe compassion sounds like code for weakness. Or maybe you've been white-knuckling your way through life for so long that the idea of being gentle with yourself feels like giving up.

Been there.

My inner monologue used to sound like a mashup of a drill sergeant and a burned-out pageant coach—intense, unrelenting, and deeply unimpressed with my humanity. And I genuinely believed that voice was helping. That if I was just hard enough on myself, I'd somehow become better. Spoiler: I didn't. Turns out, you can't hate yourself into healing. (But I gave it one hell of a try.)

Why Shame Keeps You Stuck (And How to Shut It Up)

Let's get something straight: your inner critic might be the loudmouth in the front seat, but shame is the one driving the car. Shame doesn't whisper, "You made a mistake." Shame hisses, "*You* are the mistake." It doesn't critique your behavior—it attacks your identity. And once shame moves in, it builds a

81

whole identity around unworthiness. Suddenly, you're not just struggling—you're defective. You're not overwhelmed—you're fundamentally broken.

And shame? It's versatile. It shows up wearing all kinds of outfits. It's there when you deflect compliments like they're laced with explosives. When you replay your worst moments like a Spotify playlist of personal failures. When you assume people are secretly judging you, set impossibly high standards, and then collapse under the weight of your own expectations. It's there every time you offer grace to everyone *except* yourself. And yes, it's even there when you apologize for existing after someone else bumps into *you*.

Shame fuels perfectionism, and perfectionism keeps you stuck. Because if you can't do something perfectly, why bother at all? That's the lie. And it's loud.

Shame vs. Self-Compassion: A Bloodbath (But Only One Side's Playing Fair)

If shame says, "I'm bad," self-compassion says, "I'm human." And no—self-compassion isn't about letting yourself off the hook. It's about refusing to beat yourself with it. According to psychologist Kristin Neff, self-compassion has three components. First, there's *self-kindness*—talking to yourself like you would a friend. (Unless you're a terrible friend. In which case... maybe start there.) Then there's *common humanity*, which is the radical idea that suffering isn't a personal failure—it's just part of being alive. And finally, *mindfulness*, which means noticing painful thoughts without letting them hijack your nervous system like a rogue Uber driver.

Self-compassion doesn't require you to become a walking Hallmark card. It just asks you to stop treating yourself like garbage when you're in pain.

When Self-Compassion Finally (Reluctantly) Made Sense to Me

The first time a therapist brought up self-compassion, I laughed. Loud. The full-body kind. I had spent years believing that if I showed myself any softness, I'd spiral into laziness, failure, or both. But here's the thing: I was *already* spiraling. I was knee-deep in burnout, blaming myself for not being better at pretending I wasn't. So I tried something different—barely. I didn't go full affirmation whisperer. I didn't light candles and chant into a mirror. But I did start noticing when I said things to myself that I'd never say to my kids.

That was the shift.

Little by little, I stopped being my own emotional abuser. And things started to change—not all at once, and not perfectly, but enough to realize that maybe I didn't have to earn kindness from myself. Maybe I could just... have it.

Rewriting Your Inner Narrative: A Self-Compassion Practice

Let's drag your inner critic out of the dark and into the daylight. Shame loses power when it's seen clearly. Here's a simple process to start rewriting your internal narrative.

Step 1: Name Your Inner Critic's Favorite Lines

Start by writing down the self-critical thoughts that show up when things get hard. Go ahead—pen to paper. What does the voice say? Maybe it's "I'm such a failure," or "Why can't I just get it right?" or the classic, "I should be doing better." These lines aren't truth—they're rehearsed scripts. And you don't have to keep performing them.

Step 2: Reframe Like You Would for Someone You Care About

Now take those same statements and imagine someone you love saying them. Your best friend. Your child. What would you say back? You probably wouldn't shout, "Yeah, you *are* a failure!" So don't say it to yourself either.

Try this instead: "I made a mistake, but that doesn't define me." Or, "I'm doing the best I can with what I have." Replace shame's certainty with compassion's nuance.

Step 3: Practice, Even If It Feels Cringey as Hell

Yes, this will feel uncomfortable. You'll want to roll your eyes. You'll feel ridiculous. Do it anyway. Your brain is used to one story. Changing the narrative will take repetition—and some serious awkwardness. That's normal. Keep doing it anyway. This is how you start to unhook from shame's script and write something better.

The Bottom Line: You Don't Have to Earn Your Own Kindness

Here's what I want you to remember: self-compassion isn't a prize you get for finally having your shit together. It's the fuel that *helps* you get there. You don't have to punish yourself to grow. You don't have to prove your worth by bleeding for it. You can start healing the second you decide to stop being at war with yourself.

Your inner critic might still be loud.

But you? You get to decide who holds the mic now.

Quick & Dirty Cheat Sheet

Goal:

- Shift from self-punishment to self-compassion—because you can't hate yourself into healing.

Therapy Tie-Ins:

- Kristin Neff's self-compassion model (self-kindness, common humanity, mindfulness)
- Internal Family Systems (IFS): The critic is a part, but shame is the real

puppet master

Important Reminder:

- Self-compassion isn't letting yourself off the hook.
- It's refusing to beat yourself with it.

Bonus Points:

- Flip your negative self-talk by asking, "What would I say if a loved one felt this way?"
- Then say *that* to yourself.

Next Up: TOOLKIT – Meet the Parts Keeping You Stuck

If shame is the fuel, then your inner protectors are the engine—and they've been running this show for a while. You've met the inner critic, but it's not the only part trying to keep you safe in outdated (and often wildly unhelpful) ways. In the next section, we're diving into the internal crew behind your stuck points—yes, even the ones that seem like "just your personality." Spoiler: they're not. Let's meet the parts of you that mean well, mess things up, and still deserve compassion.

TOOLKIT: Meet the Parts Keeping You Stuck

Why your brain feels like a group chat you can't leave

If you've ever debated for twenty minutes about whether to send a text or fake your own death instead—hi, welcome. You've met your parts. Most of us walk around thinking we're a single, cohesive adult with one fully functional brain. Adorable, really. But the truth? Our minds are more like an unmoderated group chat full of semi-feral personalities, all convinced *they're* the one in charge. And none of them are using their inside voices.

This is where Internal Family Systems (IFS) enters with a flashlight and a seating chart. IFS doesn't see you as "just one self" with a bunch of random issues. It sees you as a system of distinct parts—each with its own job, fear, and panic reflex. Think of it like an inner boardroom. Except the CEO is on break, the intern (hi, Self-Doubt) won't stop yelling, and the People-Pleaser keeps ordering snacks no one wants.

Spoiler: The Parts That "Sabotage" You Aren't the Problem

You know the ones. That voice that shoots down every good idea before it even forms. The doormat-with-a-smile energy that says yes to everything to avoid conflict. The catastrophizer who treats every new opportunity like a loaded weapon. These parts can be loud, obnoxious, and honestly kind of rude—but they're not the enemy. They're protectors. Outdated, exhausted, over-functioning protectors that once helped you survive something real.

86

They learned their roles in chaos and haven't been told times have changed. They're still operating off the same scripts they were handed when you were small and scared. So no, the answer isn't to shove them in a closet and pretend you're "above it." It's to meet them, understand their mission, and give them a much-needed break.

Your Internal Cast of Characters

The dysfunctional family reunion happening inside your brain.

Let's cut to the chase—these parts aren't trying to ruin your life. They're trying to keep you safe using scripts they wrote in middle school, backed by trauma, caffeine, and outdated survival data. Here's the condensed who's-who of your inner crew:

Self-Doubt (The Overthinker)

This one runs a 24/7 internal Yelp review of your every decision. It's not trying to sabotage you—it's terrified of embarrassment and thinks staying frozen is better than failing publicly. What it needs? Reassurance that discomfort isn't danger and that trying doesn't equal catastrophe.

Approval-Seeker (The People-Pleaser)

Will say yes when it means no. Will smile through resentment. Will panic if someone breathes wrong after a boundary is set. Its job is to keep you liked so you don't get abandoned. It needs to know you can survive disapproval—and that you're not auditioning for worth.

Fearful & Insecure (The Risk-Avoider)

This part is the drama queen of worst-case scenarios. It's great at preparing for chaos, not so great at living. What it needs is proof that peace isn't suspicious and trying new things isn't the same as diving into emotional quicksand.

Harmony-Seeker (The Conflict Avoider)

Keeps things "nice" at the cost of your actual needs. Bottles everything. Smiles when it wants to scream. Apologizes for existing if someone even sighs too loudly. What it needs? Permission to have hard conversations without assuming the relationship will combust.

The Moment Everything Shifted for Me

I used to treat these parts like weeds—pull them out, suppress them, shame them. But they just got louder. One day I asked my Self-Doubt part why it wouldn't shut up, and it answered (awkward). Turns out it was trying to protect 13-year-old me from ever feeling humiliated again. Every "sabotaging" part had a backstory like that. And once I listened? They softened.

They didn't vanish. But they stopped yelling.

Because now they know someone else—*me*—is finally in charge.

Mapping Your Inner Parts

Step 1: Identify Your Loudest Parts

Which of these do you recognize in yourself?

☐ The Self-Doubt Part (overthinks, fears failure)

☐ The Approval-Seeker Part (people-pleases, avoids rejection)

☐ The Fearful & Insecure Part (avoids risk, stays stuck)

☐ The Harmony-Seeker Part (conflict avoidant, emotionally suppressed)

Hint: You probably have all of them. That's not dysfunction—it's your internal system.

Step 2: Ask the Part a Question

Pick one and check in. Ask:

> *"What are you trying to protect me from?"*
> *"When did you first take on this job?"*
> *"What do you need from me now?"*

(Yes, it'll feel weird. Yes, you'll want to skip it. Do it anyway.)

Step 3: Reparent the Part

Don't silence it—soothe it. Speak to it like you would a scared kid who's been carrying too much for too long. Try:

"You were right to be scared back then, but we're not there anymore."
"You don't have to carry this alone now."
"I hear you. We're doing things differently."

Takeaway Truth: Your Parts Aren't Against You

You're not broken. You're just… crowded. Healing isn't about exiling the parts of you that feel inconvenient. It's about updating the job descriptions they've been clinging to for decades. These parts have been working overtime, unpaid, with no days off and no new training. They're exhausted. They're trying their best. And they're waiting to know if someone finally sees them and says, "You don't have to do this alone anymore."

They're not saboteurs. They're panicked toddlers with matchsticks, trying to protect you the only way they've ever known—by setting fires.

Quick & Dirty Cheat Sheet

Goal:

- Recognize your psyche isn't one voice—it's a system of protective parts, each with its own fears and survival strategies

Therapy Tie-Ins:

- Internal Family Systems (IFS): Listen to each part's story and meet it with compassion
- Parts Work: Help parts unburden and take on new, more supportive roles
- Trauma-Informed Care: Understand each part developed from a protective need

Important Reminder:

- The parts that "sabotage" you are just using outdated strategies to keep you safe
- They're not broken or bad—just tired bodyguards who need new instructions

Bonus Points:

- When a part flares up, pause and ask:
  "What are you protecting me from?"
  "What do you need from me now?"
  "What would help you rest?"
- Thank the part for trying to help—even if its methods are no longer working

Next Up: TOOLKIT – Writing Letters You'll Never Send

Now that you've met the inner crew behind the scenes—the ones who mean well but tend to set fires—it's time to give them a voice. This next chapter is where you say what you've never said. Not for closure. Not for reconciliation. For *you*. These are the letters you've written in your head a thousand times. To the ones who hurt you. The ones who left. And the version of you that still doesn't know she deserved better.

You don't have to send them.

You just have to let them exist.

TOOLKIT: Writing Letters You'll Never Send

(But Desperately Need To)

Let's be real: the idea of writing a letter to your ex, your childhood bully, or that boss who weaponized "feedback" doesn't exactly scream "healing journey." Honestly, it might make you want to gag. Sifting through old wounds is about as appealing as scheduling a root canal with extra novocaine for emotional numbness. But hear me out—this isn't about rehashing trauma for fun. It's about reclaiming control. It's about letting your voice be heard, even if the only ears it reaches are your own.

Because sometimes the most powerful thing you can do is say what needed to be said—even if it's 10 years too late and will never leave your notebook.

Healing Through Storytelling

Our brains love stories. It's how we make sense of chaos, betrayal, and the absolute mess of being human. When something deeply painful happens, our minds loop it endlessly—not like a binge-worthy drama, but more like emotional Groundhog Day. Writing takes that swirl of confusion and gives it structure. It slows the spin. It gives shape to the storm.

When you write it down, you shift from being the wounded character to the narrator with agency. You stop being just the person it happened *to* and start becoming the one who can decide how it ends. That's the kind of power that doesn't need closure—it *is* closure.

91

Emotional Release—Without the Real-Life Meltdown

Let's face it—some of these conversations are never going to happen in real life. And if they did? They'd end in disaster, disappointment, or just more hurt. Letter writing lets you say everything—ugly, raw, unfiltered—without needing the other person to be mature, safe, or even alive.

Your nervous system, bless its overworked heart, stores all that unresolved pain like a hoarder of emotional clutter. And when you finally write it down? That weight has somewhere to go. It leaves your jaw, your shoulders, your racing thoughts. And for the first time, you can breathe again.

The Science of Putting It Into Words

Let's nerd out for a sec. Putting pain into language activates the prefrontal cortex—the part of your brain that makes rational decisions, processes emotions, and calms down your amygdala (a.k.a. the fire alarm that goes off every time you smell emotional smoke). Basically, writing helps turn "AHHHH" into "Okay, this still sucks, but I get it now."

In DBT, we learn to name and notice our emotions mindfully, without judgment. Letter writing is the quiet MVP of that work. It gives structure to emotional chaos. In IFS, we talk about "exiles"—the parts of us that carry deep shame, grief, or rage. Writing is how those parts finally get to speak. And when they do, they often stop screaming.

"But I'm Never Gonna Send It..."

Perfect. That's not the point. The healing happens in the writing—not the mailing. You can burn it, read it to your dog, or stash it under your mattress next to that high school diary. What matters is that the pain leaves *you* and lands *somewhere else*.

If you ever do share it, ask yourself: "Am I doing this for connection... or to provoke a reaction?" If it's revenge, pause. If it's clarity, proceed with caution. The letter is yours. The intention behind it should be, too.

Step-by-Step Writing Exercise

Set the Scene

Grab a journal, open a document, light a candle, lock the door—whatever helps you feel safe enough to ugly cry.

Name the Wound

Start simple. What happened? Why did it hurt? No flowery metaphors needed. Just say it.

Embrace the Emotional Vomit

Swear. Cry. Be dramatic. This is not the time to be polite. No edits. No filters. Go full rage-monologue if needed.

Identify the Deepest Truth

What's really underneath all this? Do you want an apology? Acknowledgment? To be loved unconditionally? Say it, even if you'll never get it.

Find Your Power

You can't change what happened. But you *can* honor what you've learned. Let your final paragraph be a declaration: "This happened, and here's who I am now."

Decide the Fate of the Letter

Burn it? Keep it? Share it in therapy? Totally up to you. The healing already happened. The rest is bonus.

When the Letter Writes You

Here's the thing they don't tell you—sometimes, writing the letter *writes you back*. You think you're pissed at your ex, and halfway through you realize you're grieving the parent who never protected you. Or you keep writing

93

the same letter to different people, and it always ends with: "Why wasn't I enough?"

That's the gold. That's the work. Bring it to therapy. Journal about it. Text your best friend and sob into ice cream together. Just don't ignore it. Because that realization? That's where the healing cracks open.

Wrap It Up: Your Pain, Your Pen, Your Process

Writing unsent letters isn't about being dramatic or nostalgic. It's about emotional CPR. It's resuscitating the parts of you that went silent. That swallowed the truth. That still wake you up at 3 a.m. wondering what you could've said differently.

These letters are proof. Proof that *what happened mattered*. That *you* matter. And if that's not worth five pages and a few tissues, I don't know what is.

Quick & Dirty Cheat Sheet

Goal:

- Process stuck pain and reclaim your voice—not "get closure"

Therapy Tie-Ins:

- DBT: Mindful emotional processing
- IFS: Give your exiles a voice
- Narrative Therapy: Storytelling as meaning-making

Important Reminder:

- You do not have to send it
- Seriously, don't turn healing into confrontation unless it serves you

Bonus Points:

- Burn it
- Rip it up
- Share it with a therapist
- Just don't let it rot in your nervous system forever

Next Up: TOOLKIT – Healing with ADHD (When Focus Is a Myth)

So now you've met your parts and cleared some emotional clutter. But what happens when *every* part wants the mic… and your brain can't remember what it walked into the room for? That's ADHD, baby. If you've ever felt like your brain is 47 tabs open and one is playing music but you can't find which—this next chapter is for you. We're talking focus, self-worth, and why shame is NOT a motivator (even though you keep trying to make it one). Let's go.

TOOLKIT: Healing with ADHD (When Focus Is a Myth)

ADHD, overthinking, and the art of telling your thoughts to take a damn seat

If overthinking were a competitive sport, I'd have a gold medal and probably a permanent neck injury from the whiplash of spiraling so hard. And if you're here reading this? You've probably got your own award shelf. Overthinking *feels* productive—it shows up with a clipboard and sensible shoes, ready to "help." But let's not kid ourselves. It's just anxiety in a trench coat pretending to be logic.

Now throw ADHD into the mix? That's when the show really starts. You go from "What should I make for dinner?" to "Remember that awkward thing I said in 2008?" in under a second. Your brain is out here speedrunning existential dread while you're just trying to find your keys.

Overthinking + ADHD: The Chaotic Best Friends Combo

These two feed off each other like drama-loving teens at a sleepover. ADHD struggles to regulate attention, which means your brain doesn't *let go* of a thought—it builds an entire cinematic universe around it. Anxiety thrives on uncertainty. And ADHD delivers that in bulk, with bonus commentary and background noise. Executive dysfunction means you might *want* to let a thought go and still... not. It's like your mind is buffering and glitching at the same time.

And transitions? Forget it. Trying to switch tasks with ADHD feels like pushing a boulder uphill using a wet pool noodle. The result? Mental exhaustion. Decision fatigue. Emotional spirals about whether your coworker's "no worries" actually meant "I hate your guts."

How ADHD-Style Overthinking Hijacks Healing

You sit down to journal or "do the work," and your brain immediately throws a tantrum:

"Wait—am I doing this right?"

"Should I Google how to process feelings?"

"Oh my god, remember that time I called the teacher 'Mom' in third grade?"

Trying to heal with ADHD is like trying to meditate while a caffeinated toddler recites conspiracy theories in your ear. Loudly. All the time. And still expects you to remember your password for your trauma workbook login.

Tools For Managing ADHD-Style Emotional Overload

1. The Brain Dump

A.K.A. Get It Out Before You Spontaneously Combust

- Grab a notebook or app and dump *everything* circling in your brain. No order. No filter.
- Look back and sort: what's real, what's noise, what just needed to land somewhere.

Why it works: Your thoughts need a container. Otherwise, they start building drama forts in your brain like unsupervised children.

2. Call Out the Drama

Because Not Every Thought Deserves a TED Talk

- Write the thought down. ("I embarrassed myself.")

- Ask: Fact or feeling?
- Flip it: "If my friend said this, what would I say?"
- Reframe it: "Even if I was awkward, no one's obsessing over it like I am."

Why it works: You create distance from the thought and remember that *you* are not the spiral—you're the one witnessing it.

3. Use a "Thought Parking Lot"
Because Not Everything Is Urgent, Karen

- Pick a journal, note, or sticky pad labeled "Shit to Think About Later."
- Drop the worry there and move on.

Why it works: You're not ignoring your brain—you're giving it a rescheduled appointment.

4. Create a Pause Habit
Interrupt the Spiral Before It Becomes a Personality

- Set reminders: Pause. Breathe. Move.
- Ask: "Is this helping me?" If not—shift.
- Do something physical: stretch, sip water, toss your phone like you're in a breakup montage.

Why it works: ADHD brains respond to movement and novelty. Micro-interruptions create space for re-regulation.

Story Time: The 2 AM Spiral That Tried to End Me

It started with a single thought: "Did I sound weird in that conversation?" Then it mutated. "I talked too much... or not enough? Why do I never say the right amount of words? What even *is* the right amount? Should I Google that? Would Googling it make me weird? IS IT NORMAL TO GOOGLE HOW TO BE NORMAL???"

And just like that, I was wide awake at 2 a.m., planning a full personality rebrand because of a conversation no one else even remembered. The only thing I should've Googled was "how to go the fuck to sleep."

This is what unfiltered ADHD-overthinking looks like. And this is exactly why these tools matter. Because otherwise, your brain will convince you that a new zip code is the only solution to one mildly awkward exchange.

Your Turn: Try One of These Tools (Yes, Right Now)

Dump your thoughts into a notebook.
Name the spiral.
Stick the fear in a parking lot.
Stretch your arms and ask, "Is this helping?"
Even if it feels dumb, even if your brain side-eyes you, *do it anyway*. You don't need full focus—you just need one interrupted spiral.

Takeaway Truth: You Can't Think Your Way to Stillness

ADHD brains don't need more shame. They need systems. You're not lazy or broken—your brain just processes *everything* all at once, at full volume, on repeat. Don't try to silence your mind. Guide it. Make space for the chaos *and* the calm. Because even with 47 tabs open, you still deserve peace.

Quick & Dirty Cheat Sheet

Goal:

- Manage ADHD-style overthinking so you can actually heal—instead of getting stuck in mental doom scrolls

Therapy Tie-Ins:

- ADHD support: Brain dumps, thought parking lots
- Anxiety regulation: Call out dramatic thoughts, create pause habits
- IFS: Recognize when an overthinking part is panicking and step in with Self-led compassion

Important Reminder:

- You're not failing—your brain just moves at lightning speed
- You don't have to stop the thoughts—just redirect them

Bonus Points:

- Move or stretch when spirals hit
- Use short resets (30 seconds!) to help your brain stop looping
- Humor helps—so laugh when your brain throws its next weird hypothetical

Next Up: TOOLKIT: Boundaries Aren't Rude, You're Just Conditioned

When your brain is already doing the most just to function, setting boundaries can feel like another full-time job. Or worse—something that makes you feel selfish. But let's get something straight: blurry boundaries and overstimulation are a *toxic combo*. In the next section, we're ditching the guilt, unpacking the people-pleasing, and rewriting the script that says "nice" has to mean "available 24/7."

TOOLKIT: Boundaries Aren't Rude, You're Just Conditioned

How to stand your ground without immediately apologizing for it

Let's be real—boundaries are the emotional flossing of healing. Everyone says they're good for you, no one actually taught you how to do them, and if you've been people-pleasing since birth, they feel about as natural as skydiving in Spanx.

If even the thought of saying "no" makes you feel like you're pushing someone off a cliff—or lighting yourself on fire to keep them warm—you're not broken. You've just been the emotional support human in one too many trauma triangles.

Here's the reframe:

Boundaries aren't rejection. They're regulation.

They're not about building walls. They're about not leaking energy in 47 directions just to keep everyone else comfortable. That's not selfish—it's self-preservation. And yes, it'll feel awkward. It's supposed to. But that discomfort? That's not danger. That's you choosing you.

Why Boundaries Feel Like a Crime

Let's call it what it is: **guilt**.

The second you say no, your nervous system panics like you've just slapped someone's grandma. Why? Because somewhere along the line, you got the memo that saying no = being mean. That "nice" people are always available,

101

always agreeable, always apologizing for existing.

Maybe you were raised to be low-maintenance. Maybe love came with strings. Maybe you learned that speaking up got you punished—or worse, ignored.

So when you set a boundary, your brain doesn't register self-respect. It registers *threat*.

And when threat hits? Attachment style kicks in.

Attachment Styles and the Boundary Freakout

Anxious Attachment

You're terrified that saying no will make people leave—so you soften your boundary until it's basically a long-winded maybe.

What helps: Ask yourself, *"Am I protecting my peace or auditioning for approval?"* Then let their discomfort be theirs.

Avoidant Attachment

You fear closeness will mean losing yourself, so you ghost or set rigid, disappearing-act boundaries.

What helps: *"Is this boundary creating clarity—or just an excuse to disappear?"* Boundaries should build bridges, not bunkers.

Disorganized Attachment

You say no, spiral, backpedal, and rewrite the whole thing because guilt is louder than clarity.

What helps: *"Is this from fear, guilt, or grounded truth?"* You're allowed to say no without filing a 12-page justification.

Secure (or Earned Secure)

You set a boundary, breathe through the tension, and move on. It's mildly uncomfortable, not catastrophic.

What helps: Keep practicing. Even secure people feel the sting. They just don't make it a symphony.

When Validation Becomes a Trap

Setting a boundary is step one.

Not needing applause for it? That's the final boss.

The second someone looks annoyed, your brain fires up the greatest hits:

"Are they mad?"

"Did I say it wrong?"

"Maybe I should just let it go…"

And just like that, you collapse your boundary—not because it wasn't valid, but because it wasn't instantly approved.

But here's the thing:

Boundaries aren't a group project.

They don't require consensus.

And their validity isn't on the ballot.

Boundaries vs. Control: Why People Get Defensive

When someone flips out over a boundary, it doesn't necessarily mean they're toxic—it might just mean they're used to the version of you who over-functioned while they coasted.

When that dynamic shifts, it feels like *loss of access*. So they lash out. Not because you're wrong. But because they can't use you the same way anymore.

Cue the deflection remix:

- "So now I can't say anything?"
- "You're overreacting."
- "Wow… you've changed."

You end up defending the boundary instead of standing in it.

But reminder:

A boundary is not a debate. It's a decision.

Hold the Line (Without the Drama)

If they deflect: *"This isn't about that. Let's stay on topic."*
If they guilt-trip: *"I get that this is hard for you. I'm still holding my boundary."*
If they spiral: Let them. Their emotions are their responsibility. Not your clean-up job.

Boundaries Are About Self-Trust, Not Just Self-Protection

The goal isn't to make them okay with your boundary.
The goal is to stop needing them to be.
You don't need to over-explain, soften the edges, or serve your limits with a side of sugar. You just need to know they're valid. Full stop.
And yes—it'll feel uncomfortable. But that discomfort?
It's growth. Not guilt.
You are allowed to:

- Be both kind and firm.
- Protect yourself without apologizing.
- Choose peace over performance.

Your Turn: Ground Yourself in Boundary Truths

Say these. Write them. Shout them if you have to.

- "I'm not responsible for how others feel about my boundaries."
- "My worth isn't tied to anyone's comfort."
- "Saying no isn't rude. It's revolutionary."
- "I don't have to shrink to keep the peace."

Takeaway Truth: Boundaries Aren't Cruel—They're Clarity

Every time you choose yourself, the boundary gets easier.
The guilt fades. The clarity sharpens.
And what's left? Is you. Rooted. Respected. Real.
Boundaries aren't about pushing people out. They're not a velvet rope for VIPs. They're the safety rails that keep you from cartwheeling off the emotional cliff.
They're about finally choosing to stay with yourself.

Quick & Dirty Cheat Sheet

Goal:
Say no without spiraling into a shame fog.
Therapy Tie-Ins:

- **IFS**: Listen to the people-pleaser part and lead from Self.
- **DBT**: Use "interpersonal effectiveness" to protect your peace without ghosting the world.
- **Attachment Theory**: Spot when your no is panicking and stay anyway.

Important Reminder:
Boundaries are guardrails, not walls. They keep *you* from crashing—not others from reaching you.
Bonus Points:

- Say no in a low-stakes situation just to flex the muscle.
- Let people have their reactions—without contorting yourself to soothe them.
- Track the energy you reclaim every time you *don't* abandon yourself.

Next Up: TOOLKIT—Breaking the Addiction to Chaos

So, you've set the boundary. You held the line. You braced yourself for drama... and then? Silence. Space. Nothing. And instead of feeling empowered, you feel like crawling out of your own skin. That sudden stillness? That's not peace—it's withdrawal. Because when your nervous system has been wired for chaos, calm feels suspicious. Unsafe. Boring, even.

You don't want the chaos, but you don't know who you are without it. You miss the high of the crisis, the clarity that comes from reacting instead of reflecting. In the next chapter, we're unpacking why stability feels so uncomfortable, why drama masquerades as connection, and how to rewire your brain to stop confusing adrenaline for intimacy. Spoiler: it's not about being broken. It's about being detoxed from dysfunction—and learning how to live without mistaking calm for danger.

Let's build a life that doesn't need emotional fire drills just to feel real.

TOOLKIT: Breaking the Addiction to Chaos

When "calm" feels boring and "dysfunction" feels like home

If you're the type of person who gets twitchy when nothing's falling apart, feels more alive when emotions are on fire, or wonders why peace feels like wearing pants that don't fit—welcome. You're not broken. You're just a veteran of survival mode whose nervous system hasn't gotten the memo that the war is over.

This isn't "drama queen" territory. It's not about loving chaos for attention or collecting crisis like Pokémon. It's about your body, your brain, and the way they've been trained to see calm not as safety—but as the eerie quiet before the next shitstorm.

Why Your Brain Craves What's Familiar (Even When It Sucks)

Your brain's main job? Pattern recognition. It's been collecting "normal" your whole life—whether or not it was healthy. So if your early environment was a rotating carousel of emotional landmines, guess what feels like home? That's right. Emotional landmines.

Maybe your nervous system got wired on unpredictability. Maybe tension was the only reliable presence in your house. Maybe you got so used to crisis mode, you started calling it "motivation." Whatever the reason, your body adapted. It made chaos feel like comfort. And now that it's quiet? It doesn't know what to do with itself.

The Dopamine & Adrenaline Loop: Why Chaos Feels Addictive

Here's what's really happening: you're not *craving* dysfunction—you're hooked on the chemical cocktail it creates.

Stress spikes adrenaline. Then dopamine chimes in, rewarding you for surviving something that never should've been normal. That reward loop reinforces the chaos. And then when life *isn't* on fire? Your brain panics. It says, "This is weird. Let's fix it." And suddenly, you're deep-cleaning your baseboards at 1 a.m. or picking a fight just to feel something.

The high of chaos becomes the baseline. And when that high disappears? Your body acts like it's been abandoned in the desert without caffeine, carbs, or conflict.

How to Retrain Your Brain to Accept Stability

Your body doesn't need to be punished for this pattern. It needs to be *rewired*. Here's how to start:

Real-Life Regulation Tools

1. Increase Your Tolerance for Calm (Gently)

- Practice 2 minutes of stillness.
- Do low-stimulation tasks like puzzles, soft music, or easy chores.
- When the urge to start shit arises, pause.
  Why it works: Calm won't feel safe until you teach your body it *is*.

2. Replace Chaos with Controlled Excitement
Swap your go-to crisis behaviors for dopamine that doesn't require emotional whiplash.

- Last-minute panic → Short deadlines + small rewards

- Picking fights → Hobbies, challenges, or healthy competition
- Starting drama → Intense workout, thriller movie, spontaneous outing
  Why it works: Your brain still gets the stimulation it craves—just without the soul damage.

3. Rewire the Peace = Boredom Narrative
Stop telling yourself calm means flatline.

- Chaos = survival autopilot.
- Peace = freedom to choose your life on purpose.
  Why it works: You're not losing excitement—you're gaining control.

My Own Chaos Addiction (And the Bullshit I Believed)

I used to think chaos was just part of who I was. I told myself I thrived under pressure, needed the adrenaline, and just "wasn't built for stillness." But really? I was just doing what my body had always done—confusing crisis for clarity.

I'd stay in messes I didn't belong in. Start fires I had no intention of putting out. Push every deadline until my chest was tight and my brain was screaming—but hey, I was *functioning*, right?

Except I wasn't. I was in constant survival mode, mistaking pain for purpose. And calm? Calm felt like absence. Like emptiness. Like being forgotten.

It took practice—tiny, annoying, awkward practice—to see that calm doesn't mean numb. It means I finally get to *choose* how I feel, instead of reacting to whatever chaos walks in the door.

Your Turn: Chaos Detox Check-In

Ask yourself:

- When do I feel most uncomfortable with calm?

- What kind of chaos do I unconsciously create when things are going well?
- What could I try *instead* of self-sabotage when I'm restless?
  Pick one habit. One replacement. Try it once. That's enough to start rewiring the loop.

Teach your body: Peace isn't punishment. It's permission.

Takeaway Truth: Peace Isn't Boring—It's Just New

You're not meant to *earn* stillness through suffering.
You don't have to destroy something just to feel alive again.
And if calm feels wrong? That doesn't mean it is.
It means it's unfamiliar. Not unsafe.
The more you stay, the easier it gets.
And one day, peace will stop feeling like the silence before the storm—and start feeling like home.

Quick & Dirty Cheat Sheet

Goal:

- Recognize the comfort in crisis mode and retrain your nervous system to accept peace without suspicion.

Therapy Tie-Ins:

- DBT: Distress tolerance to survive the "itch" for chaos
- IFS: Meet the part that confuses adrenaline with aliveness
- Polyvagal Theory: Calm the vagus nerve to shift from fight-or-flight into regulation

Important:

- Chaos feels normal when it's all you've known. But peace doesn't mean you're boring—it means you're free.

Bonus Points:

- Practice tiny moments of stillness.
- Catch yourself when you're trying to create chaos.
- Pause. Replace. Breathe. Repeat.

Next Up: TOOLKIT: Reclaiming Your Inner Authority

So the noise is quiet. The storm has passed. And suddenly, it's just you and your thoughts—and the terrifying freedom of no longer being distracted by chaos. Now what? Now you rebuild trust in your own voice. You stop outsourcing your power to partners, parents, perfectionism. You learn what it means to *be the authority* in your own life. In the next chapter, we're handing your power back—no permission slips required.

TOOLKIT: Reclaiming Your Inner Authority

Mastering the delicate balance of self-respect and not giving a damn

Let's talk about boundaries—the ones you know you need, the ones you sort of try to set, and the ones that disappear the second someone makes a sad face. If you've ever felt like saying "no" is the emotional equivalent of drop-kicking a puppy, welcome to the club of the overly conditioned. Good news? You're not alone. Better news? You're not wrong for needing space, time, clarity, or quiet.

Boundaries are not a character flaw. They're not rude, aggressive, or cruel. They're the most honest form of self-respect you've probably never been taught. And if the only people who are mad about your boundaries are the ones who benefited from you not having any—well, that tells you everything you need to know.

This toolkit is here to break it all down: why boundaries feel awful (but aren't), the three biggest mistakes we make when setting them, what to say when your brain panics and forgets English, and how to handle pushback without spiraling into a puddle of guilt-soaked second-guessing.

Why Boundaries Feel Mean (But Aren't)

That lurch in your gut when you say "no" or the internal scramble to soften your "I can't"—it's not evidence that you're a bad person. It's just evidence that your nervous system is running on outdated software. You might've been taught that love equals sacrifice, or that advocating for yourself is somehow a threat to connection. Maybe you got praised for being low-maintenance or guilt-tripped into compliance every time you had an actual need.

If that's the case, then every boundary is going to feel like a betrayal at first. Not because it is—but because your body hasn't learned the difference between self-respect and rejection. The truth is, the right people won't crumble when you advocate for yourself. And the ones who do? That's not failure. That's clarity.

The Three Biggest Boundary Mistakes

Let's stop doing these. Immediately.

1. Over-Explaining

You don't owe anyone a TED Talk on why you can't come to their thing. A simple, "That doesn't work for me," is a full sentence. You are allowed to take up space without narrating your calendar like it's a hostage negotiation.

2. Apologizing for Existing

You are not an inconvenience for needing something. Stop apologizing for your own humanity. "I appreciate the offer, but I'll pass," works just fine. No guilt confetti needed.

3. Negotiating Your Own Limits

Saying "I can't" and then immediately backpedaling when someone pushes back? That's how you teach your nervous system that your peace is optional. Instead, try: "I said what I said." Calmly. Kindly. Unbothered.

Real-Life Scripts for When You Freeze Mid-Boundary

Let's give your brain a break and keep these ready to go.

With Family

Them: "You never call anymore."

You: "I've had a lot on my plate and I'm prioritizing my mental health. I'll reach out when I can."

113

Them: "But we're family—you should want to be around us."

You: "I care about you. And that's why I need this space."

With a Partner

Them: "Why do you need so much space?"

You: "Alone time helps me function. It's not rejection—it's regulation."

Them: "Can we talk now?"

You: "Not right now. I want to show up fully, and I need time to do that."

At Work

Them: "Can you take this on?"

You: "I don't have capacity right now."

Them: "But it's urgent."

You: "I understand, but I'm already at my limit. I won't be able to take that on."

Script Cheat Code:

If you feel the need to justify, you probably need to pause instead.

How to Handle Pushback (Without Spiraling Into Guilt)

Here's the deal: people who are used to unlimited access will not go quietly. They might try guilt-tripping, gaslighting, or pulling the "you've changed" card. That's okay. Let them squirm.

You are not here to manage their feelings. You are here to protect your own.

Classic guilt-trip tactics and how to shut them down:

- "You've changed." → "Sure have. Personal growth is wild, huh?"
- "But I need you." → "I need me too."
- "That's not fair." → "Good thing fairness isn't a prerequisite for self-respect."

Let them pout. You're done abandoning yourself to make others comfortable.

Takeaway Truth: Boundaries Are Self-Respect, Not Selfishness

You can be kind and firm. Compassionate and clear. You don't have to scream, over-explain, or apologize for putting yourself first.

Boundaries aren't about pushing people away—they're about not pushing *yourself* past the breaking point just to prove you're worthy of love.

And the next time you feel guilt creeping in, remember:

Guilt isn't truth.

Discomfort isn't danger.

"No" isn't mean. It's medicine.

Quick & Dirty Cheat Sheet

Goal:

Stand firmly in your truth and stop outsourcing your decisions to guilt, anxiety, or other people's expectations.

Therapy Tie-Ins:

- IFS: Strengthen the "Self-led" part so you're not handing over authority to anxious protectors
- DBT: Use mindfulness and emotional regulation to act from calm clarity
- Attachment Theory: Notice when fear of abandonment makes you defer—and stop doing it

Important:

Constantly outsourcing your authority = emotional self-abandonment. Your inner voice isn't a backup plan—it's your main compass.

Bonus Points:

Make *one* decision today—what to eat, how to spend your free time, what show to binge—without consulting anyone. Trust your voice. Let it lead.

Next Up: Part 3 – The Playbook

You've done the internal overhaul—mapped your parts, silenced your shame, created actual boundaries (without setting yourself on fire), and started reclaiming your own authority. Now comes the hard part: living it. In Part 3, we're taking everything you've healed on the inside and applying it to the unpredictable, exhausting, beautiful mess that is *real life*. Relationships. Holidays. Triggers. Social events with people who still think therapy is a scam. This is where healing becomes habit—and you finally start showing up like someone who belongs in their own damn life.

III

Part 3: The Playbook

Part 3: The Playbook
So, you've done the work—and now you still have to show up at Thanksgiving.
Healing in real life is messy, inconvenient, and often undermined by people who still think boundaries are "rude."
This section is your field guide for staying regulated while the world stays chaotic.

When Healing Isn't Convenient (aka, You Still Have to Show Up at Thanksgiving)

aka, You Still Have to Show Up at Thanksgiving

Let's be real: healing sounds great on paper—quiet mornings, healthy boundaries, nervous system regulation, deep insight, crying in the car while listening to a Brené Brown podcast. You've got tools now. You've done the work. You're different.

And then… you walk into your childhood home, and suddenly you're fourteen again, dodging emotional landmines while your Aunt Karen passive-aggressively comments on your weight and your uncle starts talking politics like it's a hostage situation.

Welcome to healing in environments that haven't healed with you.

This chapter is for the moments when healing isn't a retreat or a cozy journaling session. It's for when healing means holding the line while people around you pretend they don't see the fire. It's for when your nervous system says, "Hey, we've got this," but your trauma says, "Bet."

The Myth of the Ideal Healing Environment

Healing doesn't remove you from the room—it just changes how you stand in it

Here's what nobody tells you: Healing doesn't remove you from your old environment. It just gives you a different lens when you return to it.

You'll still have to sit at tables with people who gaslit you. You'll still walk into rooms where your needs were once ignored. You'll still be around

119

family who thinks "boundaries" are a new kind of disrespect.

And yeah, sometimes you still have to show up—whether it's for your kid's birthday, a holiday dinner, or a work meeting where you want to scream into the void.

Healing doesn't give you a permission slip to opt out of life. But it does give you the power to show up differently.

Why Reentering Familiar Dysfunction Feels Like a Regression

Spoiler: It's not regression—it's your trauma trying to drive

You're not broken. You're just triggered.

When you return to a place that once required survival mode, your brain goes, "Oh no. We know this place. Activate all defenses. Shut down emotional access. Cue the over-apologizer. Go, go, go!"

This isn't failure. It's a trauma-informed nervous system doing its job a little too well.

And honestly? If your healing didn't get challenged sometimes, I'd be worried you weren't actually doing the work.

Here's What You're Not Going to Do:

We don't perform healing—we protect it

- Try to educate your narcissistic cousin about emotional boundaries while passing the stuffing
- Attempt to "regulate" everyone else so you can stay calm
- Engage in petty debates just to prove how healed you are
- Over-explain your boundaries like you're defending a thesis

This chapter isn't about performing your progress. It's about protecting it.

How to Stay Regulated in Unregulated Environments

Because sometimes the healing is in the exit, not the engagement

Have an Exit Plan (or Three)

Give yourself permission to leave early, take a break, or skip altogether. Yes, even if it makes other people uncomfortable. Yes, even if someone pouts. You don't owe anyone your presence at the expense of your peace.

Identify Your Red Flags in Advance

Know what sets you off—before you get there.

"If Dad starts making jabs about therapy..."

"If Mom makes passive comments about my parenting..."

"If I get cornered in a conversation I can't escape..."

Name it. Claim it. Have a response ready—or a graceful exit line like: "I'm not going there today. Let's talk about something else."

Use the "Gray Rock" Technique for Toxic Interactions

Be unbothered, boring, brief. If someone thrives on conflict or chaos, starve them of engagement. Short, neutral answers. No emotional fuel. No invitations to dive deeper.

"Hmm."

"Could be."

"Not sure."

Smile. Sip. Exit stage left.

Stay with the version of you who did the work. Not the one they keep trying to summon with sideways comments and unresolved projection.

Anchor Yourself in Reality (Not the Role They Assigned You)

You're not who they remember. You're not who they decided you were back then. You don't have to become your teenage self just because someone uses that tone.

When You Feel Yourself Slipping Into Old Patterns

This is your cue to breathe, not break

Stop. Breathe. Ground. (Not the Instagram version of grounding. The actual body-based one.)

- Press your feet firmly into the floor
- Touch something solid and textured
- Name five things you can see
- Remind yourself: "I'm safe now. This version of me gets to choose."

Even one breath between reaction and response is progress.

My Own Version of Thanksgiving Hell

Because healing is personal—and so is self-respect

I've walked into rooms where I knew I'd be ignored. I've stayed quiet while people who hurt me made passive jokes about "how sensitive I am." I've smiled when I wanted to scream, out of habit, politeness, fear.

But now? Now I show up with an exit plan, a nervous system toolkit, and zero tolerance for emotional manipulation disguised as small talk.

I've excused myself mid-sentence. I've skipped events altogether. I've said no without guilt and yes without obligation.

Because protecting my peace doesn't make me difficult. It makes me healthy.

The Truth About Healing in Real Life

You're not doing it wrong if it's still messy

Healing doesn't mean every space becomes safe. It means you stop abandoning yourself just to make unsafe spaces feel less awkward.

You can love people and still limit your access. You can be kind and still be clear. You can show up—and walk out—on your terms.

Takeaway Truth: Peace Isn't Conditional on Their Comfort

Real healing holds when the environment doesn't

If your healing only works in ideal conditions, it's not integration—it's performance.

The goal isn't to be unbothered all the time. The goal is to notice when you're bothered—and not betray yourself in response to it.

You're not here to be palatable. You're here to be whole.

Next Up: Emotional Armor Isn't Strength (But I Get Why You Think It Is)

Surviving is not the same as connecting

It's one thing to survive Thanksgiving with your boundaries intact—it's another to realize how exhausting it is to always be the emotionally self-sufficient one. When you've spent your whole life being "the strong one," it's easy to confuse emotional isolation with resilience.

In the next section, we're unpacking the armor you've worn to stay safe, why it's no longer serving you, and how to start letting people in *without* feeling like you're losing yourself.

Emotional Armor Isn't Strength

But I Get Why You Think It Is

You know the type: the person who never asks for help, somehow becomes the designated crisis manager in every friend group, and has probably heard "I don't know how you do it!" more times than they can count.

Maybe you're that person. Maybe you had to be that person. And maybe—like me—you're starting to realize that this badge of honor is actually a 500-pound weight slowly breaking your back.

The Myth of Strength

Why the "strong one" is usually the loneliest one

Being "strong" is rewarded. Society loves it. If you're the one who never falls apart, always figures things out, and never inconveniences anyone with your messy emotions—congratulations! You're a model citizen. You might even get a gold star in Emotional Endurance (which, fun fact, is worth exactly nothing when you're alone at 2 a.m. realizing no one actually knows the real you).

But let's be real—most of us didn't choose this role.

We became "strong" because it was expected of us. Somewhere along the way, we got the message that our worth wasn't in who we were, but in how useful we could be to others.

Maybe you had to be the calm one in a household full of chaos. Maybe you learned early that expressing emotions got you ignored or punished. Maybe you were praised for being "so mature," which really just meant you learned to silence your own needs so you wouldn't be a burden. Maybe you had to prove yourself over and over again because, no matter what you did, it was never quite enough.

Either way, your emotional armor started as a survival strategy. And like all good survival strategies, it worked. Until it didn't.

The Cost of Never Letting Anyone In

If no one can hurt you, then no one can reach you either

Armor keeps you safe. But it also keeps you alone. And for a long time, that felt like a fair trade.

Except here's what happens when you operate like this long enough:

You burn out from carrying the emotional weight of everyone around you.

You get resentful because no one offers you the same support (even though you never actually let them).

You feel disconnected from people, even in relationships that are supposed to be close.

You build walls instead of boundaries, thinking they'll keep you safe—but all they do is keep you isolated.

And the worst part? You might not even realize how lonely you are—until you do.

The Approval-Seeker

The part of you that learned love was conditional

If you've ever found yourself bending over backward to be what someone else needs... If you've ever put everyone's comfort above your own... If you've ever exhausted yourself trying to prove you're enough... Then meet The Approval-Seeker.

This is the part of you that:

• Over-explains and over-justifies because you need people to understand

125

that you meant well.
- Fears disappointing others more than disappointing yourself.
- Fixes things that aren't yours to fix because being needed feels safer than being vulnerable.
- Struggles to say no because you were conditioned to believe your worth is tied to how much you can give.

The Approval-Seeker isn't here because you're weak. It's here because you learned—probably before you even had the words for it—that love, safety, and belonging had to be earned.

But here's the thing: You were never supposed to spend your whole life proving your worth.

When Hyper-Independence Stops Being a Superpower

It's not confidence—it's protection

Hyper-independence isn't strength. It's a trauma response. It's what happens when you've been let down so many times that you decide you'd rather go it alone than risk being disappointed again.

And yeah, maybe it makes you feel capable. Maybe it makes you feel in control. But it also makes you exhausted.

Because no one—not even the most self-sufficient, "I got this" person—is meant to carry life alone.

True Strength Isn't About Toughness—It's About Being Real

Vulnerability is the new flex

So if emotional armor isn't actually strength, then what is?

It's being real. It's letting people in, even when it's uncomfortable. It's knowing when to put down the shield and say, "I actually need help with this." It's recognizing that vulnerability isn't weakness—it's courage.

And honestly? It takes way more strength to be open than it does to shut everyone out.

126

Tiny Tools for Integration

For when you want to be known, but also want to ghost your therapist.

1. Try a "Micro-Ask"
Choose one low-risk request this week:

- Ask someone to grab you a coffee.
- Ask for help with something you technically could do yourself.
- Ask for emotional space instead of pretending you're fine.

Why it matters: Practicing small asks builds the nervous system's tolerance for support—without throwing you into vulnerability whiplash.

2. Interrupt the Over-Functioning Reflex
The next time you feel the urge to fix, solve, or step in:

- Pause.
- Ask yourself: "Is this mine to carry?"
- If the answer is no? Step back. Breathe. Sit on your hands if needed.

Reminder: Just because you can handle it doesn't mean you should.

3. Track the Triggers
Start a note in your phone or journal:

- When do I feel the strongest urge to "handle it all?"
- What part of me is afraid to be seen struggling?
- What do I believe would happen if I actually let someone in?

Insight: These are your Approval-Seeker cues. And no, they don't get to run the show anymore.

4. Create a Safe-to-Feel Circle

Write down 2–3 people who:

- Respect your boundaries
- Don't punish you for having needs
- Don't treat your vulnerability like an inconvenience

Practice sharing one honest thing with them this week—even if it's just: "I'm working on not carrying everything myself anymore."

Final Reminder:

Armor is built from fear. Boundaries are built from truth.
Start swapping one for the other. It'll feel wobbly at first—but over time, you'll notice the difference between being protected and being connected.

Next Up: Fine, I'll Own My Shit—But So Should You

Welcome to the wild world of accountability
Once you start peeling off that emotional armor, guess what comes up next? All the crap you've been carrying that *is* yours to own—and all the crap that *isn't*, but you've been apologizing for anyway. In the next chapter, we're diving into the wild world of accountability: how to take responsibility without self-erasing, and how to stop covering for people who refuse to clean up their own mess.

Fine, I'll Own My Sh*t—But So Should You

Because being the only emotionally mature one in the room is not a flex

So you've been doing the work. You've been reflecting, taking accountability, regulating your nervous system, managing your parts, probably over-analyzing every conversation you've ever had—and now, you're realizing something infuriating: You've been doing your healing and emotionally subsidizing everyone else's refusal to do theirs.

Let's talk about it.

When You're the Only One Owning Anything

You're carrying the weight of the dynamic—and theirs too

At some point in your healing journey, you'll hit the part where you stop blaming everyone else for your problems—and start looking inward. Which is great. Necessary. Important.

But here's the trap: When you've been conditioned to take responsibility for everything, you don't just own your part. You start owning their part, too.

Their bad mood? Probably your fault. Their defensiveness? You could've said it better. Their emotional immaturity? Maybe if you were more regulated, they'd feel safe enough to be accountable.

No. Nope. Absolutely not.

There's a difference between owning your impact and excusing someone

129

else's behavior just to keep the peace.

Accountability ≠ Self-Blame

One is healing, the other is self-erasure
Let's get clear:
Taking accountability means:

- Acknowledging when you mess up
- Apologizing when your actions hurt someone
- Being open to feedback
- Changing your behavior, not just your words

Taking all the accountability means:

- Apologizing for things you didn't do
- Managing other people's emotional reactions
- Softening your truth to avoid discomfort
- Acting like you're the only "problem" in the room

That's not growth. That's emotional self-abandonment dressed up as maturity.

You Can't Heal a Dynamic Alone

Relationships are a team sport—growth included
Listen, I'm all for personal growth. But healing is not a solo sport when it comes to relationships.
You can't:

- Communicate better *and* carry the emotional labor of someone who won't meet you there.
- Set boundaries *and* soothe someone every time they get upset about

them.
- Be self-aware *and* tolerate someone who uses your self-awareness as a way to avoid theirs.

If you're the only one growing, you're not in a relationship—you're in a performance.

The Deflection Olympics

*How people avoid owning their sht**

People who don't want to look at themselves will do anything to make sure you stay focused on you.

Classic moves include:

- **The Mirror Flip:** "You do this too, you know." (Now you're arguing about you instead of holding them accountable.)
- **The Tone Trap:** "It's not what you said, it's how you said it." (Even if you whispered it like a Buddhist monk.)
- **The Victim Pivot:** "Wow, I guess I'm just the worst person ever." (Welcome to guilt-trip central.)
- **The Emotional Hijack:** They start crying, yelling, or shutting down, and suddenly *you're* the bad guy for upsetting them.

These aren't signs of sensitivity. They're signs of accountability avoidance.

How to Stay in Your Lane (Without Taking the Whole Highway)

Protect your energy—own only what's yours

1. Start Every Check-In With This Question:

"What part of this is actually mine?"

- Not what part you're used to fixing.
- Not what part will make them less upset.
- Just: What's actually yours?

If it's not yours—*put it down*.

2. Don't Soften the Truth to Make It Easier to Hear

Sometimes the most loving thing you can do is be honest—even if it makes someone uncomfortable.

You're allowed to say:

- "This dynamic doesn't work for me anymore."
- "I need more from this relationship."
- "Your reaction doesn't mean I was wrong."
- "I'm not apologizing for that."

You don't need a permission slip to name the harm.

3. When They Deflect, Pause and Redirect

You: "I felt hurt when you dismissed my boundary."

Them: "Well, you weren't exactly nice about it."

You: "We can talk about how I said it later. But right now, I need to know if you understand why I set it."

This keeps the focus on *impact*, not *performance*.

4. Track Patterns, Not Just Apologies If someone only takes responsibility after they've hurt you—again—that's not growth. That's damage control. **Accountability isn't:**

- Saying "I'm sorry" to shut down the conversation
- Agreeing with you just to move on
- Crying, collapsing, or spiraling until you reassure them.

Accountability is:

- Naming the behavior
- Understanding the impact
- Adjusting the behavior *before* you have to beg for it

My Personal Rule: We Don't Negotiate With Deflection

Clarity over comfort—every time

I spent years over-owning. Apologizing for my tone instead of my pain. Soothing people I was actively bleeding for. Explaining myself into emotional exhaustion just to be "understood."

Now? I state it once. I don't chase clarity. I don't manage reactions. If someone can't meet me in mutual accountability, I meet myself in radical clarity. And I let that be enough.

Takeaway Truth: Shared Healing Means Shared Ownership

You're not unreasonable for wanting reciprocity

You're allowed to outgrow dynamics that refuse to grow with you. You're allowed to expect reciprocity, not just resilience. You're allowed to own your sh*t—and expect other people to do the same.

So yes, do the work. Own your patterns. Clean up your messes. But don't keep cleaning up after people who track mud through your boundaries and call it love.

Next Up: Healing on a Tuesday Afternoon with No Backup Plan

What it means to keep choosing growth—without a finish line

Taking ownership is empowering—until it's Tuesday afternoon, you're emotionally hungover, and no one's clapping for your growth.

This is the part no one posts about: the ordinary, unfiltered moments where you have to choose healing without a crisis, an audience, or a finish line.

In the next chapter, we'll talk about what it really means to keep showing up for yourself when the adrenaline fades and all you've got is your own damn courage.

Healing on a Tuesday Afternoon with No Backup Plan

Because no one claps for growth in the Target parking lot

Healing in theory? Beautiful. Transformative.

Healing in reality? You're spiraling in the Target parking lot while your nervous system decides whether to fight, fawn, or just cry next to the clearance candles.

Let's talk about that.

This chapter isn't about what healing *should* look like.

It's about what it actually looks like when you're late for work, someone sends a passive-aggressive text, your kid's having a meltdown, and your old trauma patterns are like,

"Oh hey—want us to run the show again? We remember how to protect you... poorly."

Healing Isn't a Vibe—It's a Practice

Growth starts where your comfort zone ends

You don't get to stay in your healing bubble forever. At some point, the "I've been doing the work" version of you will get invited to a family gathering, a relationship conflict, or a Monday morning—and then what?

This is where we separate the 'aha' moments from the actual rewiring.

Healing doesn't mean you'll never get triggered.

It means you notice when you're triggered—and choose not to hand the

135

mic to your inner chaos committee.

It means you know how to:

- Regulate in real time.
- Pause instead of react.
- Own your shit without over-owning theirs.
- Set a boundary before the meltdown, not after.
- Let it be messy without making it mean you failed.

When Your Nervous System Has Better Memory Than You Do

Triggers don't mean you're broken—they mean you're practicing

Sometimes everything's going fine—and then you're suddenly in shutdown mode over a tone of voice, a look, a phrase, or a weird silence.

Welcome to the part of healing where your body remembers what your mind has tried to forget.

This doesn't mean you're broken.

It means your nervous system is still practicing what safety feels like.

Here's What Helps When Reality Hits Harder Than the Inner Work

Because nervous system work doesn't end with journaling

1. Name the Part That's Activated Instead of spiraling, pause and ask:

- Who's speaking inside me right now?
- Is this my Hypervigilant Protector trying to predict disaster?
- Is it my Approval-Seeker trying to smooth things over before anyone's mad?
- Is it my Self-Doubt Part wondering if I'm overreacting (again)?

Naming the part unblends you from it. You are not the trigger. You are the one noticing it.

2. Check Your Regulation First, Not Your Morality Before you ask, "Am I being too much?"

Ask: "Am I dysregulated?"

Because half of what feels like a moral failure is just nervous system dysregulation in disguise.

You don't need to fix everything. You probably just need a glass of water, three deep breaths, and a reminder that discomfort ≠ danger.

3. Let 70% Be Good Enough Healing in real life means:

- Sometimes you catch the pattern mid-sentence.
- Sometimes you do send the emotionally-charged text—but follow up with a grounded one later.
- Sometimes you mess up, repair, and learn.

Perfection isn't the goal. Pattern recognition is.

If you did it differently than you used to? That counts. That *is* the work.

Where Patterns Still Sneak In (Even After All That Growth)

Spoiler: you're still human

With your partner: You suddenly feel abandoned over something small. (Hi, anxious attachment.)

With your kid: You go from calm to snapping in 0.3 seconds, then feel the shame spiral.

At work: You say yes to everything, then fantasize about faking your own death to avoid the project.

These aren't failures. They're flags.

They say: *You're still learning how to honor your capacity in real time.*

The Real Flex: Regulating While Triggered

It's not glamorous—but it's everything
Here's what that actually looks like:

- Walking away instead of explaining yourself into exhaustion.
- Saying "I need a minute" instead of stuffing it down.
- Choosing not to reply to that text right now—even though the itch to defend yourself is LOUD.
- Taking a deep breath and a deeper pause before you send the email.

It's unsexy. It's uncomfortable. It's annoying.

But it's where you learn that self-trust lives in the pause—not the performance.

My Reality: Integration in Motion

Progress isn't always poetic—it's often just quiet persistence
There are days I still feel like I'm failing.

Like I should be further along.

Like I should be able to show up perfectly regulated, boundaried, and eloquent even when life hits hard.

And then I remember: My healing isn't a product. It's a process.

It lives in:

- The 5 seconds I didn't lash out.
- The space I gave myself instead of chasing validation.
- The moment I said, "I need time," instead of self-abandoning for peace.

That's not weakness. That's mastery.

Takeaway Truth: Healing Doesn't Mean You Always Get It Right—It Means You Don't Pretend You Did

No finish line. No audience. Just you, choosing again.

Real-world healing isn't linear. It's gritty, reactive, sweaty, and human.

The goal isn't to be unbothered.

It's to be aware enough to stop reenacting your past just because the present felt familiar.

So yes, have the breakthrough.

But also learn to breathe through traffic, pause in hard conversations, and leave the dishes for tomorrow if your body says, *we need rest, not productivity.*

That's healing. In motion. In practice. In real life.

Next Up: Backslides, Breakdowns & Burnout

When even your best tools stop working

Even on your best healing days, life has a way of throwing you curveballs—or just wearing you down with the slow drip of "too much."

So what happens when the tools stop working, the growth feels pointless, and your nervous system files for emotional bankruptcy?

In the next chapter, we're talking about the backslides you didn't see coming, the breakdowns that cracked you open, and how to keep going when burnout whispers, *"Maybe we were better off numb."*

Backslides, Breakdowns & Burnout

Because healing doesn't erase your humanity

Let's cut the spiritual bypassing and get real: you're going to backslide. You're going to break down. You're going to burn out. Not because you're failing—but because you're human. This chapter isn't here to cheerlead you out of a hard moment with silver linings and toxic positivity. It's here to remind you that slipping back into old patterns doesn't mean your healing is fake. It means you've hit a capacity limit. And whether it feels like emotional overload, sensory overwhelm, or pure exhaustion—those limits are part of the process. Not a detour. Not a failure. Just a very normal part of doing this work.

But I Thought I Already Worked Through This?

We've all been there: a familiar reaction hits, and you immediately think, *"I thought I was past this."* You feel the frustration rising. *"Why am I reacting like this again?"* Or worse, *"Shouldn't I know better by now?"* That inner disappointment hits hard—but here's the truth: your nervous system doesn't care how many therapy sessions you've had. It cares about capacity. And when you're overwhelmed, no amount of insight can override that. Self-awareness without nervous system support is like knowing the map but having a flat tire. You might understand the why, but that doesn't always mean you're prepared for the when.

Why Healing Isn't a Linear Journey

No matter how much you want it to be

Healing doesn't happen in a straight line. It loops. It spirals. It doubles back just when you think you've figured it out. Sometimes you're gliding forward in progress, and sometimes you're faceplanting into survival strategies you swore you'd retired. But those returns to old patterns? They aren't regressions—they're invitations. Invitations to go deeper. To revisit old wounds with new tools. To see just how much you've grown by how you respond to the same trigger now compared to then. The backslide is not a betrayal. It's a bridge between where you've been and where you're going next.

Recognizing the Triggers Behind the Collapse

Burnout doesn't knock—it creeps

Backslides don't happen out of nowhere. They sneak in through the cracks of overcommitment, sleep deprivation, and unspoken resentment. You've been skipping meals and calling it "managing your time." You're saying "I'm fine" while choking back tears during a toothpaste commercial. You're handling everyone else's needs while ignoring your own. You stop doing the things that regulate you because you "don't have time." But here's the spoiler: your body *always* keeps the score. And when it's done taking on more than it can handle, it lets you know—loudly.

What a Backslide Actually Sounds Like

Hint: It doesn't sound like you

When your trauma parts go full takeover mode, the internal script gets brutal: *"Screw it. None of this healing crap is working." "Everyone else is doing better than me." "What's the point if I'm just going to end up here again?"* Maybe you tell yourself it was easier to numb out. Maybe you decide you're too much. Or maybe you quietly wonder if *you were the problem all along.* But

141

that voice isn't your truth. It's your dysregulation talking. And when you learn to recognize that voice for what it is—a flare-up, not a fact—you stop letting it define you.

What To Do When You're Spiraling

Instead of making it worse

First: pause the story. Before you start analyzing your behavior or blaming yourself, ask the most important question—*am I regulated enough to even think clearly right now?* If the answer is no, don't try to solve anything. Start with your body. Drink some water. Stretch. Ground your senses. Get horizontal if you can—seriously, lying down helps shift your nervous system out of overdrive. Then, say this out loud: *"This is a moment of regression. Not a permanent state."* Name it. Claim it. That one sentence can interrupt the shame spiral before it builds momentum.

If you've hit your limit, don't apologize—adjust. Cancel something. Delegate without overthinking how it's received. Pick the path of least resistance. This isn't about bouncing back with performance-ready resilience. This is about rebalancing. Let your nervous system lead instead of your inner critic.

And if you want clarity, get curious. Ask: *What part of me took over?* Was it the Fixer who said yes to everything? The Performer who powered through for appearance's sake? The Avoider who ghosted her support system and then spiraled in solitude? These parts aren't villains. They're overwhelmed protectors trying to keep you safe the only way they know how. You don't need to exile them. You need to meet them with compassion.

And most importantly? Don't rebuild with revenge. You don't need to overcorrect to prove you're still healing. You don't need a perfect reset. You don't need to reread every book on your nightstand. You just need rest, regulation, and enough self-trust to start again.

My Own Backslide Bingo

Because I don't write this stuff from the mountaintop

Let me be clear—I don't preach this from some enlightened high ground. I've had entire weeks where I people-pleased so hard I couldn't find my own voice. I've snapped at my kids, cried in the shower, ghosted every tool I know works, and sat in my room thinking, *Maybe I should go back to just functioning instead of feeling.* Every single time, I've had to return to this truth: healing is allowed to be inconvenient. Loud. Messy. Repetitive. Annoyingly human. But most of all—it's allowed to be nonlinear.

Takeaway Truth: You're Not Failing—You're Integrating

Backslides aren't the end. They're part of the map.

You're not broken. You're not starting over. You're integrating. The backslide isn't evidence that the work didn't stick—it's proof that you're still learning how to carry it when life gets heavy. So when you find yourself spiraling, numbing, lashing out, or shutting down, don't shame yourself for slipping. Anchor yourself in the truth that you've made it back here with more awareness than before. This isn't failure. This is feedback. And it's an invitation to come home to yourself, without performance, without pressure, and without pretending to be fine.

Next Up: SELF-DISCOVERY & CORE WOUNDS

We've made it through the fire—now let's look at what's underneath it

You've faced the fallout. Now it's time to face the foundation. This next section doesn't ask for perfection—it asks for honesty.

We're diving into the roots of your relational patterns, attachment wounds, inner critics, and survival-driven parts that shaped how you show up (or shut down). These worksheets aren't here to fix you. They're here to help you *see* you. Because once you name what's been running the show, you don't have to keep living on autopilot.

143

Let's pull back the curtain. Let's find out why you really are the way you are.

IV

SELF-DISCOVERY & CORE WOUNDS

Before you can heal it, you've gotta name it. This section helps you unpack the deeper roots of your patterns—attachment wounds, critical inner voices, and the parts of you that got stuck in survival mode. No sugarcoating, just clarity.

WORKSHEET: So… Why Are You Like This in Relationships?

An honest breakdown of your attachment style (and how to stop letting it run the show)

You're not "too much." You're wired for survival. Your brain got really good at staying safe, even if it meant sabotaging connection. But guess what? You can unlearn the panic and relearn how to feel safe—without reenacting your childhood every time someone doesn't text back.

Start Here

Quick step before we dive in

If you haven't already, head over to traumasolutions.com/attachment-styles-quiz and take the full quiz. It'll give you the clearest read on your dominant attachment style. Then come back here, find your style, and let's untangle the mess with some clarity, compassion, and a little side-eye at your survival instincts.

Anxious Attachment

"I just need to know we're okay—like, constantly."

How This Shows Up:

You second-guess texts. You reread tone. You apologize for things you didn't even do—just to keep the peace. You care deeply, but it often feels like too much... even to you.

- You worry people will leave—even when they say they won't.
- You overanalyze silences, pauses, and delays.
- You abandon your own needs to avoid being abandoned.
- You feel "needy," try to shrink it, or let it spill and feel ashamed later.

What You Crave:

Reassurance. Emotional closeness. Proof you matter.

What You Fear:

Being left. Being ignored. Being replaced.

Mini-Toolkit: Moving Toward Secure

- **Regulate Before You Reach Out:** Before you send "Are you mad at me?" take a few deep breaths. Soothe your nervous system before reaching out for connection.
- **Create Internal Reassurance:** Build an inner voice that reminds you, "I'm okay—even if they need space."
- **Practice Interdependence:** Ask for what you need. Not from panic, but from clarity. You're allowed to want connection without apologizing for existing.

Avoidant Attachment

"I'm fine. I don't need anything. Also, why doesn't anyone ever show up for me?"

How This Shows Up:

You crave connection but hate the vulnerability it requires. You pull away before others can. Independence isn't just your vibe—it's your armor.

- You feel smothered when things get too close—even if you care.
- You assume no one can meet your needs, so you stop having them.
- You go quiet during conflict or emotion-heavy conversations.
- You secretly want intimacy but fear being trapped by it.

What You Crave:

Space. Autonomy. Low-pressure connection.

What You Fear:

Being controlled. Losing yourself. Needing anyone.

Mini-Toolkit: Moving Toward Secure

- **Name What You Need (Silently Counts):** You don't have to share it out loud yet. Just start identifying what's going on inside instead of skipping the emotional part.
- **Try Safe Closeness in Small Doses:** Let someone in just a little. 5% more vulnerability won't kill you—it might even help.
- **Replace "I Don't Care" with "I'm Uncomfortable":** It's not apathy, it's armor. Call it what it is so you can start working with it.

149

Disorganized Attachment

"Come close!—No wait, don't!—Ugh, why does this always happen?"

How This Shows Up:

You feel like a human contradiction. You want love. You push it away. You crave safety. You run when you find it. You're constantly torn between clinging and fleeing.

- You swing between anxious and avoidant like it's an Olympic sport.
- You sabotage closeness when it feels too intense.
- You don't trust love to last, but you keep chasing it.
- Your inner child and inner protector are at constant war.

What You Crave:

Unconditional love. Safety. Someone who stays.

What You Fear:

Being abandoned. Being exposed. Being controlled.

Mini-Toolkit: Moving Toward Secure

- **Build Dual Awareness:** Practice holding both truths—"I want closeness *and* I feel scared."
- **Work With Your Parts:** Use IFS to explore the child who wants love and the protector who fears it.
- **Create Consistency With Yourself:** Before you trust others, become someone *you* can count on. Predictability builds safety—even if it starts internally.

Secure Attachment

"I can be close without losing myself. Weird, right?"

How This Shows Up:

You're comfortable in connection and separation. You communicate clearly, handle feelings like a grown-up, and don't need drama to feel alive.

- You don't spiral when someone needs space.
- You can express needs *and* hear no without combusting.
- You set boundaries and offer support without keeping score.
- You don't play games, chase, or ghost. You're an adult. Imagine that.

What You Crave:

Mutuality. Respect. Authenticity.

What You Fear:

You still feel fear—but it doesn't run the show.

Mini-Toolkit: Staying Secure (Because Triggers Still Exist)

- **Don't Assume You're "Done" Healing:** Secure doesn't mean unshakeable. It means you return to center faster.
- **Offer Co-Regulation, Not Over-Functioning:** Be a safe presence without absorbing someone else's work.
- **Notice When You Slip:** Triggers happen. The key is how quickly you realign.

Final Note

You don't need to become some perfectly secure robot to have good relationships. You just need **awareness, self-responsibility**, and **a willingness to grow**.

Oh, and maybe less doomscrolling. That too.

WORKSHEET: How I Learned to Attach Like That

A no-shame breakdown of how your relationships trained your nervous system

Let's be real—your attachment style didn't just *happen*. It was shaped by the people who were supposed to love you, hold you, and teach you what safety felt like. This worksheet is about spotting those patterns, not pointing fingers. Because awareness isn't about blame—it's about power.

Step 1: Your First Blueprint — Early Caregivers

Where the map was drawn, even if it didn't make sense

Think back to your earliest relationships. The ones that whispered (or screamed), "This is what love feels like." Those whispers became your wiring.

- **What did love feel like growing up?**
- Was it warm and responsive? Cold and conditional? Chaotic and confusing? Use real words, not sugarcoated ones.
- **When you were upset, how were your feelings handled?**
- Did someone hold space for you, or did you learn to shut it down fast? Were you comforted, ignored, punished, or told to "be strong"?
- **What messages did you get about needing help or being vulnerable?**
- Complete the sentence: *"If I asked for help, I was met with..."*
- **Who wasn't safe to go to—and why?**

153

- Sometimes the most unsafe people were also the ones who said "I love you" the most. That's not a contradiction—it's conditioning.

Pause and Notice: *Your attachment system learned more from what people* did *than what they said. That includes silence, unpredictability, and emotional abandonment dressed as discipline.*

Step 2: Adolescent Reinforcement

When the foundation started showing cracks—or deepened

Your teen years weren't just a hormone-fueled blur. They were another chapter in your attachment story. This is when you started learning how the world responded to your emotions, independence, and worth.

- **What were your key relationship dynamics as a teen?**
- Think of friendships, romantic interests, mentors, and even authority figures. Who saw you? Who disappeared when you needed them most?
- **What did you learn about trust and closeness during that time?**
- Did you learn to open up—or shut down? To perform and please—or to isolate? Be honest about what survival required.

Mini Insight: *Many of us started performing our way into acceptance here. If your safety depended on being "easy to love," your attachment style probably took shape accordingly.*

Step 3: Adult Patterns

Where the ghosts of old dynamics start dressing up as new people

This is the part where your nervous system gets loud. Because by adulthood, your early scripts are either running on autopilot—or getting called out. (And maybe both.)

- **How do your current relationships reflect—or reject—those early**

templates?

- Are you reenacting the same dynamics with new names and faces? Do you choose emotionally unavailable partners—or *become* the emotionally unavailable one? Do you overfunction to stay connected or push people away before they get too close?

Real Talk: *Your nervous system isn't sabotaging you. It's following an outdated script that once kept you safe. But guess what? Scripts can be rewritten. And this is your permission slip to start.*

WORKSHEET: My Trauma Isn't the Problem—The Silence Is

A reclaiming statement for the version of you who stayed quiet too long

Let's get one thing straight: you weren't overreacting. You weren't "too sensitive." And you weren't making it up. The real wound wasn't just what happened—it was the crushing weight of having to go through it alone, unacknowledged, or disbelieved.

This worksheet helps you break that silence. It's not for debate. It's for truth-telling. And for finally letting go of the shame that was never yours to carry.

Your Reclaiming Statement

Write it. Read it out loud. Tape it to your mirror. This is your truth.

Fill in the blanks below to create a powerful reclaiming statement that honors what happened—and what you're no longer willing to stay silent about.

Something happened when I was _____
(age, season of life, or situation)
It made me feel _____
(scared, alone, ashamed, furious, invisible... be specific)
But no one _____
(believed me / helped me / noticed / gave a damn)

156

So I learned to _____
(shut down / perform / stay silent / be perfect / carry it all)
And for a long time, I believed _____
(it was my fault / I was broken / I had to earn love / I deserved it)
Now I know the truth: _____
___

(You get to write this part without shame. Claim it.)

Declaration

Because truth doesn't need a permission slip

I'm allowed to own my story without justifying my pain.

I'm allowed to name what hurt me—even if it makes other people uncomfortable.

I'm allowed to stop carrying the weight of other people's denial.

My trauma isn't the problem. The silence is. And I'm done staying quiet.

You don't owe anyone a watered-down version of your story.
Your truth is not too much—it's yours.

Reflection: What Owning My Story Makes Possible

Because naming the past clears space for your future

Naming what happened doesn't trap you in the past—it gives you the power to choose what's next. This section helps you see what shifts when you stop pretending everything was fine.

1. **Now that I've named my truth, what do I no longer have to carry alone?**
   (*Guilt? Shame? Other people's reactions? Something else?*)
2. **What becomes easier when I stop pretending I'm fine?**
   ☐ Saying no

157

☐ Asking for help

☐ Feeling my emotions without shame

☐ Trusting myself

☐ Setting boundaries without over-explaining

☐ Other: _____

3. **What does owning my story make possible in my relationships?**
   (*Think honesty, reciprocity, filtering out the people who can't hold your truth*)

4. **How will I remind myself that my voice matters—especially when doubt creeps in?**
   (*Mantra, action step, support system, self-talk—something you'll actually use*)

You're not broken for having a story.

You're brave for telling it.

And you're powerful for choosing what happens next.

WORKSHEET: The Inner Critic Debrief

Get curious—not crushed

Your inner critic isn't just a jerk for sport. It's a scared part of you that learned somewhere along the way that shame = safety. That if it yells loud enough, maybe it'll keep you from failing, falling, or feeling pain again. The goal here isn't to drown it in glittery affirmations—it's to get curious about what it's really trying to say (and who taught it to say it that way).

1. What Did My Critic Say?

Verbatim. No editing. No softening.

Write it down exactly as it showed up in your head—yes, even if it's mean, dramatic, or ridiculous. That voice thrives in the shadows. We're dragging it into the light.

2. Whose Voice Does This Sound Like?

Parent? Teacher? Yourself at fifteen?

Think about the tone, the timing, and the content. Whose approval were you chasing? Who made you feel like "not enough" was just your natural state?

3. What Fear Might This Be Covering Up?

The critic yells to protect what's tender.

Shame is often just fear in a mean outfit. What's underneath this voice—failure, rejection, abandonment, not being good enough?

4. Is This Helping Me or Hurting Me Right Now?

Be honest about the impact.

The inner critic claims it's here to "motivate" or "keep you in check." But how's that working out for you?

5. What Does This Part of Me Actually Need Instead of Shame?

Because criticism without care isn't protection—it's harm.

Check what feels true right now. Then consider offering it to yourself, without needing permission.

☐ Reassurance
☐ Rest
☐ Encouragement
☐ Boundaries
☐ Permission to not be perfect
☐ Other: _____

Final Thought

The inner critic isn't your enemy. It's a scared protector using shame as armor. But you're not that same vulnerable version of you anymore. You've got tools now. And what this part needs most is to know—you've got this.

WORKSHEET: Meet the Glass Box Part

Write a letter to the silenced, unseen part of you—the one still waiting to be heard

This is for the version of you who was punished for crying. Ignored for needing. Mocked for feeling. The one who learned to survive by staying quiet. You don't have to fix her. You don't have to rescue her. You just have to acknowledge her.

Write the Letter

A template for truth-telling, not performance

You can write this in your journal, speak it aloud, whisper it in the dark, or just hold the words in your chest. There is no wrong way to show up for the part of you that was left alone in the silence.

Dear [insert age or name for your Glass Box part],

(*Example: "Dear 13-year-old me" or "Hey, Silent One—I see you now."*)

I know you felt...

(*Describe their emotional reality. Afraid? Invisible? Ashamed? Too much? Too alone?*)

You didn't deserve...

(*Name the harm. What was withheld, denied, punished, or unseen?*)

What I wish someone had said to you back then is:

What I still want you to know now is:

You are not...

(*Finish the sentence: "You are not broken." "You are not alone." "You are not to blame."*)

161

You are...
(*End with truth: "You are worthy." "You are allowed to speak." "You are safe with me."*)
I promise to...
(*How will you show up for them now? Speak kindly? Set boundaries? Stop pretending you're fine?*)
With love,
The you who's finally listening

> *You can't change what happened to her.*
> *But you can stop abandoning her now.*

Get to Know Your Glass Box Part

Visualize. Name. Connect.

This isn't about dragging up memories or forcing a healing moment. It's about honoring the part of you who adapted by disappearing.

What name, age, or label feels right for this part?
(*Examples: "13-year-old me," "The Quiet One," "Muted & Moody," "Glass Box Girl"*)

If you picture this part, what do you see?
Describe their body language, clothing, facial expression, surroundings. Or sketch them if you're visual. No art degree required.

Extra Credit: Grab a blank sheet or open up your favorite design app (hi, Canva nerds) and bring them to life—stick figure, collage, mood board... whatever makes them real to you.

What emotion does this part carry the most?
- ☐ Shame
- ☐ Fear
- ☐ Rage
- ☐ Hopelessness
- ☐ Numbness
- ☐ Other: _____

What does this part most want from you now?
(Be honest—attention? Reassurance? Permission to take up space?)

Reflection: How This Part Still Shows Up Today

She's not in the past. She's still in the room—waiting for you.

You may have grown up. But this part? She's still stuck in the silence. Until you reconnect, she'll keep pulling the strings behind the scenes—especially in moments of rejection, shame, or fear.

When do you notice this part taking over?
(Think: situations where you shut down, freeze, over-explain, or feel invisible)

What triggers remind her it's not safe to be seen or heard?
(Certain tones of voice? Conflict? Rejection? Being dismissed or talked over?)

What would it look like to protect her without silencing yourself?

(A boundary? Speaking up gently? Letting her know it's okay to be scared while still showing up?)

Reconnection isn't about fixing her. It's about freeing her.
She was never the problem. The silence was.

WORKSHEET: Parts Mapping

Get those internal protectors out of your head and onto the page

You've got a whole internal crew—some are loud, some are sneaky, some are exhausted. They're not trying to ruin your life. They're trying to protect you, even if their methods involve control, panic, people-pleasing, or total shutdown.

This worksheet helps you name who's been running the show, what they're afraid of, and what they *actually* need. You're not here to evict them—you're here to lead them.

Example: The Over-Responsible Jenga Part

The one who thinks if they don't hold everything together, everything will collapse

- **Part Name:** The Over-Responsible Jenga Part
- **Role / How It Shows Up:**
  Takes on too much, plans for every possible failure, stays calm while dying inside, apologizes for things I didn't do just to keep the peace.
- **What This Part Is Trying to Prevent:**
  Chaos. Criticism. Failure. Disappointment. Anything falling apart.
- **What This Part Actually Needs Instead:**
  To know I can drop a few blocks and the whole tower won't crash. Permission to rest. Help. Reassurance that my worth isn't tied to holding it all together.

Now You Try

Repeat for each part as needed
Part Name:

Role / How It Shows Up:
(*What this part does, says, or feels like when it takes over*)

What This Part Is Trying to Prevent:
(*The fear or threat it's protecting you from*)

What This Part Actually Needs Instead:
(*Not panic. Not control. Try: reassurance, rest, boundaries, clarity, support*)

Part Name:

Role / How It Shows Up:

What This Part Is Trying to Prevent:

What This Part Actually Needs Instead:

Part Name:

Role / How It Shows Up:

What This Part Is Trying to Prevent:

What This Part Actually Needs Instead:

> *You don't need to silence your parts.*
> *You need to listen to them.*
> *Then lead them—with clarity, not control.*

V

NERVOUS SYSTEM & BODY AWARENESS

Your body always knows—most of us just learned to ignore it. This section helps you recognize the signs of stress, shutdown, and survival mode so you can stop white-knuckling through life and start responding with awareness instead of autopilot.

WORKSHEET: How Do I Know I'm Dysregulated?

Become a regulation detective—your body's leaving clues

Dysregulation doesn't always scream. Sometimes it whispers through clenched jaws, forgotten meals, or four hours lost to Instagram reels. You might not even realize you're dysregulated until you've hit the emotional wall (or snapped at a barista for breathing too loud).

This worksheet helps you catch the signs earlier—*before* your system goes into full-body protest.

Instructions

Pattern awareness, not perfection

Use this tracker for the next three days. Log physical, emotional, and behavioral signs of nervous system dysregulation as they show up. Don't try to fix it all—just *notice*. Awareness is regulation's quiet sidekick.

DAY ONE

Physical Clues *(check all that apply)*
- ☐ Tight chest
- ☐ Shallow breathing
- ☐ Jaw clenching
- ☐ Racing heart

171

- ☐ Stomach knots
- ☐ Restless legs
- ☐ Headache
- ☐ Numbness or zoning out
- ☐ Other: _____

Emotional Clues

(*Overwhelmed? Irritable? Numb? On edge?*)

Behavioral Clues

(*Scrolling black hole? Over-apologizing? Snapping at people? Forgetting to eat?*)

What helped—or could have helped—me regulate today:

DAY TWO

Physical Clues (*check all that apply*)
- ☐ Tight chest
- ☐ Shallow breathing
- ☐ Jaw clenching
- ☐ Racing heart
- ☐ Stomach knots
- ☐ Restless legs
- ☐ Headache
- ☐ Numbness or zoning out
- ☐ Other: _____

Emotional Clues

Behavioral Clues

What helped—or could have helped—me regulate today:

DAY THREE

Physical Clues *(check all that apply)*
- ☐ Tight chest
- ☐ Shallow breathing
- ☐ Jaw clenching
- ☐ Racing heart
- ☐ Stomach knots
- ☐ Restless legs
- ☐ Headache
- ☐ Numbness or zoning out
- ☐ Other: _____

Emotional Clues

Behavioral Clues

What helped—or could have helped—me regulate today:

You don't have to wait until you're spiraling to check in.

Awareness is the first regulation tool—and your body's already talking.

Start listening.

WORKSHEET: Top 5 Body Clues I Ignore Until It's Too Late

Spoiler: Your body tried to warn you. You ghosted it. Let's fix that.

Dysregulation doesn't come out of nowhere. Your body sent the early alerts. You just...declined the call. Again. This worksheet helps you track the patterns you bulldoze past so you can catch them *before* you're rage-cleaning at 2 a.m. or crying over a sock that betrayed you.

Instructions

Think back. Get honest. Find the pattern.

Think about your last few dysregulation spirals. What showed up *first*—before the full crash? These are the clues your body whispered. Let's make sure you don't ignore them next time.

The First Thing I Notice (But Usually Dismiss):

The Physical Symptom I Downplay Until It's Screaming:

The Behavioral Red Flag I Pretend Is "Just a Phase":

175

The Emotion I Try to Outrun:

The Clue That Always Means I'm About to Snap (But I Still Ignore It):

Now What?

Let your future self breathe.

Write one way you'll pause or respond differently next time these clues show up.

"When I notice _____,

I'll choose to _____

instead of spiraling."

> You don't need a meltdown to earn rest, regulation, or support. Your body is whispering long before it screams—start listening while it's still whispering.

Regulation Reset Menu

Pick one. You don't need a ritual—just a reset.

When your system is fried and your body's flipping every internal breaker, don't overthink it. Just choose something doable. Simple is powerful when you're on edge.

MOVE (Gently or Weirdly—Doesn't Matter)

☐ Shake out your arms for 30 seconds like a damp dog

☐ Go outside and walk one loop around the block

☐ Stretch your spine and yawn (fake yawns count)

☐ Dance to one loud, angry song

☐ Push against a wall with your full body for 10 seconds

SOOTHE (Without Judgment)
☐ Run warm or cold water over your hands

☐ Wrap up in a blanket like a burrito and breathe

☐ Smell something grounding (peppermint, lavender, coffee)

☐ Use a heating pad or ice pack on your chest or back

☐ Press your feet into the floor and narrate five things you feel

UNCLUTTER YOUR MIND
☐ Write a brain dump of every "what if" swirling in your head

☐ Say out loud: "I am not in danger. I am overwhelmed."

☐ Do the "What's Actually True Right Now?" script (p. __)

☐ Set a 5-minute timer to do nothing and just be still

☐ Name 3 people who love you—and imagine telling one of them how you feel

RECONNECT TO THE PRESENT
☐ Name: 5 things you see, 4 you can touch, 3 you hear, 2 you smell, 1 you taste

☐ Look at something green (plants, trees, whatever) for at least 30 seconds

☐ Hold something weighted (pillow, dog, gallon of milk—no one's judging)

☐ Put one hand on your chest, one on your stomach, and count to 10

☐ Watch your dog (or a video of one) just being a dog

You don't need a crisis to use your tools.
You just need permission—and here it is.

WORKSHEET: "What's Actually True Right Now?"

A reality check script for anxious spirals and nervous system freakouts
When your nervous system flips the emergency switch and your brain starts writing worst-case fanfiction, you need something solid to hold onto. This worksheet helps you slow the spiral, separate the fear from the facts, and give your body a way back to baseline.

Instructions

Use this script during or after a trigger. No perfection required.
You're not trying to win a logic debate here. You're trying to reconnect to what's *real*—and calm the alarm bells going off in your head and body.

Trigger

What just happened that set off your alarm bells?

My Initial Thought

What story did my brain immediately tell me?
(Be blunt. Don't edit it to sound wise or rational.)

What I Know Is True

Ground it. What's *actually* real, right now? What evidence do I have?
(*Not assumptions. Not future-casting. Just present truth.*)

What My Body Needs

What would help my nervous system settle right now?
- ☐ Deep breath
- ☐ Movement
- ☐ Soothing touch (blanket, heating pad, etc.)
- ☐ Getting outside
- ☐ Space or time to reset
- ☐ Water or snack
- ☐ Other: _____

Example

Trigger:

They didn't text back for hours.

My Initial Thought:

They're mad at me / I messed something up / I'm being rejected.

What I Know Is True:

They've been busy lately. They haven't said anything is wrong. I have no proof of conflict.

What My Body Needs:

To put down my phone, go outside for five minutes, and breathe into my chest instead of spiraling in my head.

> *Anxious thoughts feel urgent.*
> *Truth feels steady.*
> *Come back to what's true—and let your body catch up.*

WORKSHEET: From Defense Mode to Real You

Trace your top survival strategies and how they were adaptive

You didn't ruin yourself. You adapted. Every wall you built was a response to something unsafe—something your body and brain worked overtime to survive. This worksheet helps you track where your defenses came from, what they've protected you from, and what they're costing you now.

Timeline Reflection: Childhood → Teen → Adult

Track the shape-shifting armor you built to survive

Use this reflection to notice patterns. Some defenses never left. Others evolved into new ones as your environment changed. You weren't being difficult—you were staying alive.

Childhood

Defense Mechanism:

(Example: People-pleasing, going mute, perfectionism, being "the good kid")

What It Protected You From:

(Rejection, chaos, punishment, being invisible, emotional neglect...)

181

What It Costs Now:

(Loss of self, resentment, chronic anxiety, burnout, lack of boundaries...)

Teen Years

Defense Mechanism:

(Example: Anger, rebellion, emotional shut-down, overachievement, caretaking)

What It Protected You From:

(Feeling powerless, unsafe, unseen, unheard, or unworthy)

What It Costs Now:

(Isolation, impulsivity, shame spirals, distrust in relationships...)

Adulthood

Defense Mechanism:

(Example: Hyper-independence, sarcasm-as-shield, control issues, avoidance)

What It Protected You From:

(Vulnerability, failure, disappointment, repeating old trauma)

What It Costs Now:

(*Disconnected relationships, decision fatigue, emotional numbness, chronic stress...*)

And maybe—just maybe—the emotional price of being the easy one isn't worth the Costco-sized pack of resentment you've been hauling around like it's a good deal. You didn't choose these defenses to be difficult—you chose them to survive. And they worked. But now that you're safer, now that you know more—it's okay to outgrow them.

Compassion first. Change second.

Integration: Okay, So Now What?

Start reclaiming your power—gently

You've named the armor. Now let's talk about what's underneath. You don't have to throw out every defense overnight. You just get to decide what still serves you—and what doesn't.

Which defense still feels necessary—and why?

(*Is there a part of you not ready to let go? What would it need to soften?*)

What's one defense that's doing more harm than good now?

(*Pick one—not all. Go where there's readiness, not pressure.*)

What could you replace that defense with?

(*A boundary instead of people-pleasing? Self-expression instead of shutting down?*)

183

Who would you be underneath all that armor?

(*Let yourself imagine. Who are you when you're not in defense mode?*)

Integration isn't about becoming someone new.
It's about remembering who you were before the world told you to be someone else.

VI

SCRIPTS & COMMUNICATION CHEAT SHEETS

Words are hard—especially when you're triggered. These scripts take the guesswork out of what to say (to yourself or someone else) when you're spiraling, shutting down, or trying to set a boundary without exploding.

CHEAT SHEET: Secure Scripts for Anxious, Avoidant & Disorganized Days

Say the thing—but say it in a way your nervous system won't regret later

You don't have to *feel* secure to *practice* secure.

These scripts help you show up with clarity, boundaries, and emotional honesty—even when your attachment system is in full-blown "protect at all costs" mode.

The goal? Communicate like the real you underneath the spiral.

When You're Feeling Anxious

You're not needy. You're craving connection—and that's human.

Try This:

> *"I'm noticing I feel anxious about our distance. I don't need a fix—just some reassurance would help."*
>
> *"I want to check in—not because I think something's wrong, but because I value our connection."*
>
> *"This is hard for me, and I'm working on not making assumptions when I feel disconnected."*

When You're Feeling Avoidant

Space isn't the problem—avoidance of vulnerability is. Practice reaching for connection without abandoning yourself.
Try This:

> *"I'm feeling overwhelmed and need some space—but I'll reconnect once I've grounded."*
> *"It's hard for me to open up, but I want to try. I'm asking for patience, not pressure."*
> *"I tend to shut down when I feel too exposed. I'm not withdrawing—I'm regulating."*

When You're Feeling Disorganized

Push-pull isn't sabotage—it's protection. Let the chaos speak honestly.
Try This:

> *"I'm having mixed feelings right now—I want closeness, but I'm scared too. Can we move slowly?"*
> *"Sometimes I react before I understand what I'm really feeling. I'm trying to pause and figure it out."*
> *"I know I push and pull sometimes. I'm not trying to confuse you—I'm learning how to feel safe in connection."*

When You're Practicing Secure Attachment

You don't need to be perfect to show up grounded. You just need to be honest and respectful—of them and you.
Try This:

> *"I care about you, and I also need to honor my boundaries. Both are true."*
> *"I don't need you to fix this—I just want to feel like we're in it together."*
> *"I can hold space for both of us, and I trust we'll figure it out."*

These scripts aren't magic spells.
But they are neural pathway practice.
The more you say them, the less your nervous system freaks out when you do.

CHEAT SHEET: Scripts for Talking to Your Inner Chaos Crew

These aren't just quirks—they're protectors. And they're exhausted.

Every part of you that gets "too loud," "too much," or "too shut down" has a reason for being there. These aren't bad habits or broken pieces—they're your nervous system's security team, doing the job they were trained to do. Poorly. But still.

This cheat sheet helps you talk to them like they're real (because they are), instead of yelling at them to chill while they hijack your entire day.

The Self-Doubt Part

Wants to keep you from looking stupid or failing. Thinks second-guessing everything = safety.

Common Triggers: Decision-making, visibility, being seen as "too much" or "not enough"

Try saying:

> *"I hear you. You're trying to protect me from being wrong or judged. But I've got this now."*
>
> *"You don't have to run the show today. I'll take the risk—we're safe enough."*
>
> *"Thank you for double-checking. I'll move forward, even if it's not perfect."*

The Approval-Seeker

Convinced that being liked = survival. Will people-please until you disappear.
Common Triggers: Conflict, rejection, disapproval, silence from others
Try saying:

> *"I know you're afraid of losing connection. But we don't have to abandon ourselves to keep others happy."*
> *"Being real is safer than being liked. You don't have to work so hard."*
> *"What if we let people love us for who we actually are?"*

The Harmony-Seeker

Panics when anyone's upset. Believes peace is worth any price—even your needs.
Common Triggers: Tension, unmet expectations, big emotions (theirs or yours)
Try saying:

> *"It's okay if someone's uncomfortable. We can stay grounded and still be kind."*
> *"We're allowed to disagree. We don't have to fix everything."*
> *"Keeping the peace can't keep costing us our truth."*

The Fearful & Insecure Part

Still thinks you're a kid waiting to get hurt again. Doesn't trust anyone to stay.
Common Triggers: Intimacy, vulnerability, love that feels too safe (and therefore suspicious)
Try saying:

> *"You're not overreacting—you're remembering. But we're not in danger now."*
> *"You don't have to go it alone. I'll stay with you while we feel this."*

191

"Love isn't the threat it used to be. We can let good things happen."

The Shutdown Protector

Pulls the plug on feelings, connection, or effort when things get overwhelming.

Common Triggers: Conflict, overstimulation, vulnerability hangovers
Try saying:

"I see you trying to shut it all down. Can we pause instead of disappearing?"
"You're allowed to rest. But you don't have to ghost ourselves."
"We can feel a little bit of this without going numb."

The goal isn't to "get rid" of these parts—it's to earn their trust. Once they believe you're actually in charge? Game. Changer.

Now It's Your Turn: Meet Your Own Inner Crew

Start building trust with the voices in your head (in a totally normal, healing way)

My Part's Name:
(*Make it specific, weird, funny, or heartfelt. Whatever helps you spot it next time.*)

What It's Trying to Protect Me From:
(*What is it afraid will happen if it doesn't step in?*)

What Triggers It Most Often:
(*People, situations, sensations, or emotions*)

What I Want to Say to This Part:

(Kind, direct, grounded. No "go away"—we're building trust here.)

(Repeat this section for as many parts as needed. If your inner world feels like a dysfunctional committee meeting—good. That means you're paying attention.)

Every part of you has a reason.
You don't have to like them all—but they deserve to be heard, understood, and gently updated.

CHEAT SHEET: Critic-to-Compassion Scripts

Respond to your inner critic without spiraling, apologizing, or shrinking

You don't need to drown your inner critic in glittery affirmations you don't believe. You just need to interrupt it with grounded truth. These scripts help you respond with boundaries, not backlash.

This isn't about pretending you don't have doubts. It's about showing up anyway—and reminding your critic who's in charge.

When Your Critic Says:

"You're such a mess. Why can't you just get it together?"
Try Responding With:

> *"I'm doing the best I can with the capacity I have right now—and that's enough for today."*

When Your Critic Says:

"No one's going to take you seriously. You're a fraud."
Try Responding With:

> *"Imposter syndrome isn't proof I don't belong. It's proof I'm stretching into something new."*

When Your Critic Says:

"You always screw things up. Of course you did this wrong."
Try Responding With:

"Mistakes don't erase my worth. I can be imperfect and valuable."

When Your Critic Says:

"If you were better/more/less [insert toxic standard], they wouldn't leave you."
Try Responding With:

"My worth doesn't hinge on being 'just right' for someone else. I deserve love without performing for it."

When Your Critic Says:

"Don't even try. You'll just fail again."
Try Responding With:

"Failure isn't fatal. And not trying guarantees I stay stuck. I'd rather grow."
Self-compassion isn't weakness.
It's a nervous system regulation strategy.
You don't have to silence your critic. Just speak a little louder—with truth.

Emotional Boundary Script Builder

Because "no" is a complete sentence—but sometimes you want more options
Setting boundaries isn't about being cold—it's about being *clear*. You're not rude for protecting your peace. You're regulated. And sometimes, you want more than just a mic drop "no"—you want language that reflects your capacity, your limits, and your self-respect.

Use these sentence stems to build boundaries that don't invite debate—or self-betrayal.

Choose Your Script Starter

Pick one based on the situation—or your nervous system's current bandwidth
"That's not going to work for me because..."
(Use when you want to give brief context—but not open the floor for negotiation)

> *"That's not going to work for me because I'm protecting my time right now."*
> *"That's not going to work for me because I've got too much on my plate, and I'm not willing to burn out over it."*
> *"That's not going to work for me because I've committed to honoring my bandwidth—even if it disappoints someone."*

"I'm not available for..."
(Use when you need to name your limit with zero wiggle room)

> *"I'm not available for that kind of conversation right now."*
> *"I'm not available for emotional dumping without consent."*
> *"I'm not available for taking on more responsibility than is mine."*

"Let me think about that and get back to you."

(Use when you feel pressure to say yes but need space to check in with yourself first)

> *"Let me think about that and get back to you—I'm trying not to agree to things from a place of guilt."*
> *"Thanks for asking. I'll need a little time to see if I have the capacity."*
> *"I don't want to give you a half-hearted yes, so let me check in with myself first."*

Bonus: End-of-Boundary Power Moves

Add one of these if you feel the pushback coming

> *"Thanks for understanding." (translation: this is not up for debate)*
> *"That's the best I can offer right now."*
> *"I hope you can respect that—even if it's not what you were hoping for."*
> *"If that doesn't work for you, I understand—but I won't be changing my answer."*

Boundaries aren't walls—they're **doors with locks**.
You get to decide who comes in, when, and under what conditions.

197

Boundary Guilt Reframe

Because even when you set the right boundary, guilt shows up wearing a halo

You're not mean. You're not selfish. You're not too much. You're just finally telling the truth about what you can and can't give.

This worksheet walks you through the guilt spiral—so you don't undo your boundary out of shame.

1. What boundary did I set?

(Be specific. What did you say no to? What did you stop tolerating?)

2. What guilt is coming up right now?

☐ I feel like I let them down
☐ I'm scared they're mad at me
☐ I feel like I should've just sucked it up
☐ I think I overreacted
☐ I'm worried I'll lose the relationship
☐ Other: _____

3. Whose expectations am I trying to meet right now?

(Family script? People-pleasing reflex? Internalized "Good Person" rulebook?)

4. *What's actually true about this boundary?*

☐ It was honest
☐ It was respectful
☐ It was necessary
☐ It was overdue
☐ It was hard, but I did it anyway
   "The boundary I set was _____ and it mattered because _____."

5. *What would it feel like to let the guilt exist—without letting it steer?*

(You don't have to like guilt. Just don't confuse it for a moral compass.)

Quick Reframes to Borrow When You're Spiraling

"This guilt doesn't mean I did something wrong—it means I did something different."
"I'm not responsible for someone else's disappointment with my limits."
"Holding a boundary is an act of self-respect, not disrespect to others."
"Their reaction is not proof I was wrong—it's proof they're used to me abandoning myself."
"The guilt will pass. The boundary is worth keeping."

Guilt is just the echo of old conditioning.
You don't owe it your silence.

VII

INTEGRATION & RELAPSE PREVENTION

Healing isn't linear, and falling apart doesn't mean you failed. This section gives you tools to navigate setbacks, hold your boundaries when others don't get it, and recommit to yourself—even when it's messy.

WORKSHEET: Backslide Survival Plan

For when you're spiraling and need a soft, sarcastic landing

Healing isn't linear. It's a messy loop-de-loop with snacks, shutdowns, and those charming moments where you forget every coping skill you swore you had mastered. This worksheet is your emergency exit from the shame spiral—*no perfection required.*

1. What Just Happened?

Name the chaos. No overthinking. Just own the moment.

> *"I just _____ and now I feel like I'm back at square one."*

2. Which Part of Me Took Over?

Identify your inner chaos gremlin with honesty and maybe a little humor.

(Was it the Avoider? The Over-Apologizer? The Angry Teenager? The One Who Ghosts Their Therapist?)

3. What Would Future Me Want Me to Remember?

Channel your wise, regulated self—or fake it 'til you make it.

"Future Me would say: _____
___"

4. What's One Kind Thing I Can Do Next?

Choose one. That's enough.

☐ Put the phone down and breathe

☐ Eat something that isn't rage-snacks

☐ Step away from the self-blame monologue

☐ Text someone safe (or your dog counts too)

☐ Take a nap, a walk, or a shower

☐ Other: _____

A backslide isn't proof you failed.
It's proof you're still in process—*and still showing up.*

Backslide Bounce-Back Menu

Tiny ways to recover without pretending you didn't just spiral

This isn't about "getting back on track." It's about letting your nervous system know it's okay to keep going. You're not broken. You're just human—with a brain that occasionally misfires and a body that needs help catching up.

Regulate the Body

So your brain stops lying about how doomed you are

☐ Breathe in for 4, hold for 4, out for 6. Repeat until your jaw unclenches.

☐ Cold water: hands, face, neck—reset the system.

☐ Move your body a little: shake it out, stretch, walk in a circle.

☐ Sit still and say out loud: "I'm here. I'm safe enough. I'm not in the past."

Repair with Yourself (Not the Critic)

☐ Write one sentence that starts with "I'm proud of myself for…"

☐ Whisper "I still deserve good things"—even if you don't believe it yet.

☐ Do your favorite comforting thing (yes, snacks count).

☐ Close your eyes and picture Future You giving this moment a shrug instead of a breakdown.

Rewrite the Narrative (Because You Didn't Fail)

☐ "This was a dysregulation moment, not a character flaw."

☐ "I'm still healing, even on the days I feel like a dumpster fire."

☐ "I've come back from worse than this. I'll come back again."

☐ "Messy doesn't mean meaningless."

Pick a Micro-Win and Call It Progress

☐ Send one honest text instead of ghosting everyone

☐ Get vertical (off the floor or couch = win)

☐ Drink a glass of water and make eye contact with your dog

☐ Take a 5-minute break from self-loathing

☐ Say: "I'm not fine, but I'm not failing either."

The bounce-back doesn't have to be dramatic.
It just has to be true.
Choose one kind thing. That's enough for today.

WORKSHEET: When My Healing Pisses People Off

Reframe the guilt. Hold the line. Keep healing anyway.

Let's be honest—growth doesn't always get applause. Especially from the people who benefitted from your silence, your compliance, your burnout. When you start honoring yourself, some people *will* get uncomfortable. That doesn't mean you're doing it wrong. It means you're finally doing it *honestly*.

This worksheet helps you process the pushback—without shrinking.

1. What Boundary Did I Set?

(What did you say no to, stop doing, or stop pretending was okay?)

2. How Did They React?

☐ Guilt-tripping
☐ Silent treatment
☐ Defensiveness
☐ Accusing me of being selfish, cold, dramatic, etc.
☐ Trying to renegotiate the boundary

☐ Other: _____

Describe the reaction in your own words:

3. What Part of Me Feels Guilty—and Why?

(Is it your people-pleaser? Approval-seeker? Inner child who just wanted peace?)

4. What Would I Say If I Believed My Needs Mattered Too?

Let your empowered self speak—*even if it's just a whisper.*
"If my needs mattered, I'd say: _____
___"

Reframe the Guilt: Borrow One If You Need It

"They're allowed to have feelings. I'm allowed to have boundaries."
"Their discomfort doesn't mean I did something wrong."
"I didn't betray them—I stopped betraying myself."
"If protecting my peace makes me the villain, I'll live."
"I'm not responsible for managing someone else's reaction to my healing."

Healing isn't always harmonious.
Sometimes it's loud, messy, and met with resistance.
Set the boundary anyway.

Self-Validation Script Builder

Because sometimes the only person who gets it... is you.

You don't need applause or approval to know you're growing. You need truth. This tool helps you name your wins and hold your ground—even when no one else claps.

1. What Did I Do That Deserves Validation Today?

(Held a boundary? Chose rest? Told the truth? Didn't spiral?)

2. What Did It Cost Me to Do That?

☐ Discomfort
☐ Guilt
☐ Risking rejection
☐ Internal resistance
☐ Fear of being misunderstood
☐ Other: _____
Describe the emotional toll in your own words:

3. What Would I Say to a Friend Who Did the Same Thing?

(Now say it to yourself.)

4. What Truth Do I Want to Stand In—Even If No One Else Sees It Yet?

"Even if no one claps for me, I still know: _____
____"

Sample Self-Validation Scripts to Borrow Anytime

"That was hard—and I did it anyway."
"I don't need outside permission to trust my own limits."
"I can be proud of myself even if no one else understands."
"This doesn't have to look graceful to still be growth."
"I didn't make it easy. I made it honest."

Self-validation isn't self-indulgent.
It's self-leadership.
Clap for your damn self.

Post-Boundary Recovery Checklist

You did the hard thing. Now do the soft thing.
　Boundaries are emotionally expensive. This checklist helps you recover from the hangover—without undoing the work.

STEP 1: Tend to the Body

☐ Drink a glass of water like you mean it
☐ Shake it out (arms, legs, jaw—whatever's holding tension)
☐ Press your feet into the floor and feel your body supported
☐ Put your hand on your chest and say: "I'm safe. I'm allowed."
☐ Rest your eyes or step outside—no stimulation for 2 full minutes

STEP 2: Tend to the Emotion

☐ Name what you're feeling (even if it's "weird and messy")
☐ Let yourself cry, vent, or journal without fixing it
☐ Say: "I don't have to be okay with their reaction to still stand by my boundary."
☐ Remind yourself: **Discomfort is not danger.**

STEP 3: Remind the Critic Who's in Charge

☐ "It's okay that I feel guilty—this is new, not wrong."
☐ "People can be disappointed. I can still be proud."
☐ "Boundaries aren't mean. They're maintenance."
☐ "I don't need to soften the truth just to stay likable."

You don't owe anyone a guilt hangover just because you finally chose yourself. Take care of the version of you who used to stay silent.

WORKSHEET: The Healing Contract (With Yourself)

No, it's not legally binding. Yes, it's still powerful.

This isn't a promise to be perfect. It's a vow to keep showing up—for yourself.

To stop abandoning the version of you that's trying so hard to heal.

To choose truth over performance. Compassion over shame.

And to remind yourself: even when it's hard, you're still worth the effort.

Sign your name. Say it out loud. Tape it somewhere you'll see it.

I Commit To...

(Choose a few. Or write your own.)

☐ Honoring my limits even when others don't understand

☐ Feeling my feelings instead of numbing them

☐ Listening to my body, even when my brain wants to override it

☐ Asking for what I need (even if my voice shakes)

☐ Letting rest be productive

☐ Other: _____

When I Fall Back Into Old Patterns, I'll...

(Not "if." When. Because healing is human, not linear.)

☐ Offer myself compassion instead of shame

☐ Ask: "What do I need right now?" instead of "What's wrong with me?"

211

☐ Use my tools instead of my coping mechanisms (or at least try)
☐ Reach out instead of isolating
☐ Remind myself: I don't have to earn the right to begin again
☐ Other: _____

I Am Healing Not to Be "Better" But to Be…

"I am healing not to be 'better,' but to be _____."

Signature: _____

Date: _____

> *You don't need a breakthrough.*
> *You just need to mean it.*
> *This isn't about proving anything.*
> *It's about returning to yourself—again and again.*

The Compassion Clause

Signed by: Me, a Human Who's Still Healing
I agree to forgive myself for the parts of healing I didn't get "right."
For the days I shut down instead of speaking up.
For the times I reverted to old patterns, lashed out, avoided, numbed, or forgot every damn tool I've ever learned.

I agree to treat myself with compassion, especially when I fall short of my own expectations.
I agree to stop using perfection as proof that I'm "worthy" of peace.
I agree to keep going, even when it's messy, slow, or doesn't look like progress to anyone else.

Signed: _____

Date: _____

You don't have to be flawless to be healing.
You just have to be willing to come back to yourself.

Letter Template: The Reconciliation You May Never Send

Letter to Someone I'm Reconciling With (Even If They'll Never Read It)
This is not for them.
It's for *you*.

Closure doesn't always come with a conversation, a confession, or an apology.
Sometimes it comes with telling the truth—to yourself.
This letter is your space to speak what was silenced.
Not for revenge. Not for performance. For *release*.

Dear _____,
(*Name, label, or just "the one who hurt me / let me down / didn't show up"*)

Here's what happened that still lives in my body:

This is how it made me feel, even if I never said it out loud:

What I wanted from you (and maybe still do):

214

Here's what I've carried because of it:

And here's what I'm choosing to release—
Not to excuse it, but to free myself from it:

You don't have to say anything.
I'm not writing this for a reply.
I'm writing this to reclaim my voice, my space, and my healing.

Signed,
Me—finally telling the truth

This letter doesn't need to be sent to be real.
Speaking your truth is reconciliation enough.

Worksheet: What Forgiveness Actually Means (And What It Doesn't)

Redefining forgiveness so you don't gaslight yourself
Forgiveness isn't pretending it didn't happen.
It's not minimizing the pain, bypassing the anger, or spiritually polishing a red flag into a lesson.

Forgiveness, in the context of healing, is about **freeing yourself**—not excusing them.

This worksheet helps you sort out what forgiveness looks like *for you*—if, when, and how you choose to offer it (or not).

Let's Start With the Truth

What happened that I'm being told I should forgive?
(*Be direct. No sugarcoating. No justifying their behavior.*)

What I Used to Think Forgiveness Meant
(*"If I forgive, then I have to..."—finish the sentence with the old belief*)

216

What Forgiveness Doesn't Mean

Check all that resonate:

- ☐ Saying it was okay
- ☐ Letting them back into my life
- ☐ Forgetting what happened
- ☐ Denying the impact
- ☐ Rushing myself into peace
- ☐ Giving up my anger before I'm ready

What Forgiveness Can Mean

(You define it. Choose the ones that feel empowering—leave the rest.)

- ☐ Releasing the need for closure from someone who may never give it
- ☐ Untangling myself from the shame they left behind
- ☐ Making space in my nervous system for *my* life—not just the aftermath of theirs
- ☐ No longer allowing what they did to decide what I believe about myself
- ☐ Setting them down—not out of kindness, but because I'm tired of carrying them

Optional: A Forgiveness Statement (That You Don't Have to Mean Today)

*"I forgive you not because it didn't hurt—**but because I'm ready to heal without carrying it.**"*

"I may not be ready to forgive. But I'm ready to start releasing the hold this has on me."

Reflection: What Forgiveness Looks Like (For Me)

Because your healing deserves your definition.

If I were to forgive, it would look like:

(Boundaries? Internal release? Never talking to them again? Be honest.)

217

What would change in me—not for them—if I forgave in my own time, on my own terms?

Forgiveness isn't always the destination.
*Sometimes it's just **not carrying the weight** so you can move forward—with yourself.*

Worksheet: How to Move On Without Closure

Because sometimes you don't get the ending—but you still get to move forward
You don't need their apology to begin again.
You don't need their version of the story to validate your own.
Closure isn't something you wait for—it's something you **create**.

This worksheet is about grieving the door they never closed—and walking through your own anyway.

1. What Did I Hope They'd Say or Do That They Never Did?

(Be honest. Write the apology, explanation, or gesture you wish had come.)

2. What Questions Do I Still Catch Myself Wanting Answers To?

("Why wasn't I enough?" "Did they even care?" "Was any of it real?")

3. What Truth Do I Know—Even Without Their Confirmation?

(Not what they said. Not what they denied. What do YOU know was real?)

4. What Would I Say If I Knew They'd Never Truly Hear Me?

(Your uncensored truth. No expectation of a response. Just your voice.)

5. What Am I Still Carrying That Isn't Mine?

(Shame, self-blame, guilt, doubt, responsibility for their behavior—name it.)

Closure You Give Yourself

Choose the one that feels most powerful to say (or write your own):
"I deserved clarity, but I won't let their silence define my worth."
"They don't have to acknowledge the harm for it to be real. I lived it."
"I wanted closure from them. I'm giving it to myself."
"Even without their apology, I am allowed to heal, release, and move on."
"They don't get the final word. I do."

Now What?

Moving on doesn't mean forgetting. It means re-centering.
What does moving on look like in this season of your life?
☐ Not rereading the old messages
☐ Letting go of the need to prove your side
☐ Saying their name less—and your own more
☐ Making space for what's next, not what could've been
☐ Other: _____

You may never get closure *from* them.
But you can create resolution *within* yourself.
That's not giving up—it's choosing peace over permission.

VIII

Bonus Tools & Resources

Here's your all-in-one cheat sheet—every script, tool, and practice from the book in one place. No fluff, no extra scrolling. Just the healing strategies you actually want to come back to when life hits the fan.

TOOLBOX RECAP: A Cheat Sheet of Every Practice, Script, and Survival Hack

A Cheat Sheet of Every Practice, Script, and Survival Hack
You made it.

Through the wreckage, the WTFs, the over-apologizing, the dissociation, the breakthroughs, the "maybe I *am* the problem" moments, and the occasional urge to light your life on fire and move to a cabin with no Wi-Fi. (Relatable.)

This section is here to say:

You're not starting from scratch anymore.

This is your personal healing arsenal—stuff that actually works.

Come here when you're spiraling. When you're trying to explain trauma to someone who thinks boundaries are "mean." Or when you just need a reminder that you're not broken.

TOOLKIT: Teaching Your Body You're Safe

- **Orienting:** Look around the room and name 5 neutral or pleasant things.
- **Pendulation:** Shift gently between a difficult memory/sensation and a resourcing anchor (blanket, scent, image). Dip in, dip out.
- **Vagus Nerve Support:** Humming, gargling, cold water, deep exhales— signal safety from the body up.

- **Body-Led Safety Anchors:** Weighted blankets, soft textures, slow rocking. Let your body lead.
- **Reality Check Script:** Ask, *What's actually true right now? What's the threat? What power do I have?*
- **Safe Touch & Movement:** Feet on the floor. Hand on chest. Move something—*even if it's just your pinky toe.*

TOOLKIT: The Inner Critic Isn't the Problem—Shame Is

- **Call It by Name:** "That's shame talking. Not truth."
- **Trace It Back:** Whose voice is this? (Parent? Ex? Internalized standard?)
- **Give It a Job Title:** "Director of Perceived Failure Prevention."
- **Replace Criticism with Curiosity:** Ask, *What's the unmet need behind this shame?*

TOOLKIT: Meet the Parts Keeping You Stuck

- **Self-Doubt:** Afraid of being wrong, usually born from not being believed.
- **Approval-Seeker:** Confuses being liked with being safe.
- **Fearful & Insecure:** Needs backup plans for its backup plans.
- **Harmony-Seeker:** Avoids conflict at the cost of your needs.

To work with them:

1. Ask what they're afraid of.
2. Validate it.
3. Reassure them: *"I've got this now."*

TOOLKIT: Healing with ADHD (When Focus Is a Myth)

- **Body Before Brain:** Regulate first—then try to think.
- **Interrupt the Spiral:** Stand up. Change scenery. Say "STOP" out loud.
- **Micro-Tasks:** Break it down until it's ridiculous. "Open email" is valid.
- **Visual Timers & Anchors:** Alarms, sticky notes, color codes = life.
- **Let 'Good Enough' Be the Win:** Showing up, even scattered, counts.

TOOLKIT: Reclaiming Your Inner Authority

- **Pause the Polling:** Stop asking what others would do. Ask *yourself*.
- **Notice Externalizing Language:**
- "Should I...?" → "Do I want to...?"
- "Is it okay if...?" → "Here's what I've decided."
- **Somatic Yes/No:** Body tightens = no. Body softens = yes.
- **Confidence = Skill, Not Emotion:** Decide → Survive → Trust builds.

TOOLKIT: Fear Is a Liar (But Damn, It's Convincing)

- **Unblend from the Fear:** "A part of me is scared"—that's *not* all of you.
- **Build a Fear Profile:** What does it believe? What's the worst-case?
- **Anchor to the Present:** Orient. Ground. Fear thrives in fantasy.
- **Ask:** *What would I do if I didn't feel afraid?*

TOOLKIT: Tiny Tools for Integration

- **Mini-Check-Ins:** "What do I feel? What do I need?"
- **30-Second Grounding:** Wiggle toes. Touch something cold.
- **Internal Notes App:** "Hey team, I know we're overwhelmed. I've got us."
- **Reverse Mapping:** Track what helped after the fact, so you can use it sooner next time.
- **Gentle Self-Honesty:** "I'm not okay, but I'm showing up." That counts.

TOOLKIT: Scripts, Boundaries & Brave Conversations

- **Boundary Script (Clear + Kind):**
- *"I care about our relationship, and I need to be honest about what's not working for me."*
- **Accountability Script (No Over-Explaining):**
- *"I'm open to repair when you're ready to take responsibility. Until then, I need some space."*
- **Closure Script (When They Won't Change):**
- *"I'm choosing peace over proving my point. I wish you well, but I'm done explaining myself."*
- **Self-Validation Script:**
- *"It makes sense that I feel this way. I don't need others to agree for it to be valid."*

Final Note: You're Not Broken—You're Rewiring

This toolbox isn't about becoming someone new.

It's about remembering who you were before the world taught you to abandon yourself

Come back here anytime

Not because you're behind, but because you're **building muscle memory**.

And muscle memory isn't failure.

It's **practice**.

IX

Mapping the Wreckage

Sometimes healing starts by seeing the mess for what it is—no fixing, just noticing. This worksheet is your bird's-eye view of the emotional debris you've been carrying. Use it to name what hurt, what protected you, and what you're ready to release. No judgment, just a map.

"Wreckage Map" Worksheet

Track where the emotional debris is hiding. No judgment, just awareness.
This isn't about fixing yourself.
It's about seeing the sh*t you've been hauling around so you stop tripping over it in the dark.
These patterns? They're not random. They're rehearsed.

This worksheet helps you map the wreckage—so you can finally stop running into it on autopilot.

1. What Parts of You Feel Most "In Charge" Day-to-Day?

(*Think: the hyper-competent overachiever, the people-pleaser on Red Bull, the ice queen who pretends not to care.*)
Who's driving the bus most often—and how do you know?

2. What Triggers Your Shutdown, Freakout, or Overfunctioning?

(*List the people, situations, or emotions that hit your internal panic button.*)
(*Bonus points: label the response—fight, flight, freeze, or fawn.*)

3. Where Did These Patterns Actually Come From?

(*First memories, old environments, relationships that trained you to survive this way. What felt "normal" growing up that maybe... wasn't?*)

These aren't flaws. They're adaptations.
This worksheet isn't about blame—it's about clarity.
The more honest you get, the more power you take back.

Reflection: What Now?

You found the wreckage—now let's figure out what to do with it.
Awareness isn't the end goal. It's the entry point.
This is how you stop reenacting old scripts and start *responding*—on your terms.

1. Which Part of You Needs Some Damn Rest?
(*The over-functioner? The manager? The inner control freak?*)
What would it look like to give it a break—without everything falling apart?

2. What's One Trigger You Want to Meet Differently Next Time?
(*Pick one. Name it. And ask: How could I pause here? What would support look like—not shame?*)

3. What Kind of Safety Does Your Nervous System Need More Of?
☐ Internal safety (self-trust, emotional regulation)
☐ External boundaries (with people, screens, stressors)
☐ Physical calm (sleep, routine, breath, movement)
Choose one—and name what that support could look like today:

You don't have to bulldoze your way through healing.
Start by witnessing your patterns *without flinching.*
That's where the real power starts.

X

Your Healing on Speed Dial

Whether you're ready to deep dive with a therapist, binge a podcast that hits too close to home, or just need support at 2AM, this section's got you. Here's your shortcut to trusted resources, recommended reads, and the real-deal pros who can help you keep going when the book closes.

Therapy & Coaching Guide

Because healing solo is brave—but getting help is smarter.

Not all therapists are created equal. Some will change your life. Some will just nod for 45 minutes and send you a bill. And some will accidentally re-traumatize you while handing you a stress ball and asking, "But have you tried gratitude?"

So let's cut through the noise. Here's how to find support that actually supports you.

How to Choose the Right Therapist

Without Settling

Start Here: What's Your Goal?

Are you trying to…

- Process trauma?
- Navigate a life transition?
- Learn emotional regulation tools?
- Understand your inner parts?
- Stop spiraling and start functioning?

Knowing your "why" helps you filter out the fluff and find someone with the actual skills to help.

Look For:

- Trauma-informed care (bonus points if they understand chronic or developmental trauma)
- C-PTSD experience (especially important for chronic, developmental trauma)
- Attachment-based therapy (essential for reworking relational patterns)
- Internal Family Systems (IFS) (for parts work—hi, Glass Box Girl)
- Dialectical Behavior Therapy (DBT) (emotional regulation, boundaries, and crisis management)
- Somatic Therapy (body-based work that speaks the language of your nervous system)
- Brainspotting or EMDR (for trauma resolution beyond talk therapy)
- Neurodivergence-informed approaches (ADHD, autism, sensory overwhelm)

Red Flags to Watch For:

- Overfocus on "positive thinking" or "just let it go"
- Minimizing or invalidating your experience
- Misunderstanding trauma responses or neurodivergence
- Pushing past your boundaries rather than honoring them
- Consistently feeling worse after sessions

Therapy vs. Coaching

Know the Difference

Therapists are trained and licensed professionals who help you process trauma, understand your past, regulate your nervous system, and build emotional safety. They can diagnose, offer clinical insight, and support deep healing.

Coaches are often certified but not licensed. They focus on mindset, future vision, habits, and accountability. A good coach can help you move forward when you're not in active crisis or trauma recovery mode.

Choose Therapy When:

- Healing from trauma or C-PTSD
- Needing support with emotional or nervous system regulation
- Exploring internal parts, reparenting work, or attachment wounds
- Addressing invalidating past experiences needing safe, reparative interactions

Choose Coaching When:

- You've done some inner work and want to shift into action
- Ready to build new habits, goals, or systems
- Seeking structure, reflection, and accountability
- Needing forward momentum—not deep emotional excavation

Pro tip: The dream team is one of each. A trauma-informed therapist for root work and a strategic coach for real-world application? Unstoppable.

Where to Look

Without Spiraling into Decision Fatigue
Best Therapist Directories:

- **Psychology Today** – Large database; filter by insurance and modality
- **TherapyDen** – Inclusive, trauma-aware, LGBTQ+ affirming
- **Open Path Collective** – Affordable options for out-of-pocket payments
- **Inclusive Therapists** – Identity-safe, anti-oppressive care
- **Local universities/nonprofits** – Reduced-cost therapy from supervised grad students

Search Tips:
Use keywords like:

- "IFS"

- "C-PTSD"
- "Somatic therapy"
- "DBT"
- "Religious trauma"
- "Neurodivergent-affirming"

What to Say When Reaching Out

Therapist Inquiry Script:

> *"Hi, I'm looking for a trauma-informed therapist who works with nervous system regulation and attachment patterns. I'm especially interested in [IFS, DBT, somatic work, etc.]. Do you have availability for a consultation?"*

Reminder: You're interviewing them too. You're allowed to ask questions, request what you need, and walk away if the vibe is off. (That's not "difficult"—that's discernment.)

Questions to Ask During the First Session

Don't just sit there trying to impress them with how self-aware you are. Ask real questions:

- "What's your approach to trauma and nervous system regulation?"
- "Are you familiar with IFS or parts work?"
- "How do you handle rupture or misattunement in the therapy relationship?"
- "Do you offer practical tools, or is your work more exploratory?"
- "What happens if I dissociate or shut down in session—how would you respond?"

If they look confused, dismissive, or start defending generic trauma training—thank you, next. You're hiring someone to help untangle your emotional spaghetti, not someone to nod politely and bill you.

A good therapist won't just fit—they'll be honest, grounded, and secure enough to say, "Hey, I might not be your person," without flinching.

And once you do find the right one? They'll still call you out—but it won't feel like an attack. It'll feel like someone finally saw behind your defenses and said, "I get why you built these walls... and I'm here to help you take them down brick by brick."

Because healing isn't about being coddled—it's about being met.

Therapy Homework That Doesn't Suck

If your therapist suggests "just notice your thoughts" or "try meditating" without more depth, you deserve better.

Real Healing Practices to Use In or Out of Sessions:

- Bring your IFS parts map to explore who's running the show
- Use your integration journal to track nervous system shifts
- Share boundary scripts and get feedback
- Review thought spirals and practice reframing
- Track body-based safety cues (tension, calm, grounding tools)
- Write a letter to your inner protector and read it aloud in session
- Use real-life ruptures as practical case studies

Healing isn't linear, but it's easier with someone trained in trauma, nervous system science, and emotional safety—someone who won't just toss mindfulness buzzwords at your survival instincts.

Final Takeaway

You're Allowed to Need Help

You're not broken for needing support. You're not weak for wanting guidance. You're someone who's survived—and finally wants to stop surviving and start living.

Whether therapy, coaching, or a messy mix of both:

- Get what you need.
- Ask for more.
- Walk away from the mediocre.

Healing is hard enough without having to educate your therapist too.

Quick-Access Crisis & Support Resources

Because healing is hard—and sometimes, you need backup.

Whether you're mid-panic spiral, emotionally unraveling in a Target parking lot, or just need a reminder that you're not alone—this section is here for you. These resources aren't a replacement for therapy, but they can absolutely be a lifeline when your nervous system is screaming, *"I can't do this alone."*

Immediate Crisis Support

United States

988 Suicide & Crisis Lifeline

Call or text **988** for 24/7, confidential support. Prefer to type? Visit 988lifeline.org/chat to connect with a crisis counselor.

Crisis Text Line

Text **HOME** to **741741** for immediate support from a trained counselor.

Veterans Crisis Line

Call **988**, then press **1**, or text **838255** for veteran-specific support.

The Trevor Project (LGBTQ+ Youth Support)

Call **1-866-488-7386** or text **START** to **678678** for free, affirming support.

RAINN (Sexual Assault Hotline)

Call **1-800-656-HOPE (4673)** or chat at hotline.rainn.org.

In an Emergency—Call 911

If you or someone else is in immediate danger, or there's a medical or safety emergency, call **911**. Let the dispatcher know it's a mental health crisis so they can send the right kind of help. It's okay to be direct: *"This is a mental health emergency—I need someone trained in crisis response."*

Canada

Talk Suicide Canada
Call **1-833-456-4566** or text **45645** (available 4 p.m. to midnight ET).
Crisis Text Line (Canada)
Text **686868** for immediate support.
Hope for Wellness Help Line (Indigenous Support)
Call **1-855-242-3310** for culturally sensitive support.
Kids Help Phone
Call **1-800-668-6868** or text **CONNECT** to **686868**.

Not Ready to Call? Start with Someone You Trust

You don't have to be in full crisis to ask for help.

Asking for help doesn't mean you've failed. Even I—someone who literally wrote a book on healing—have had to call a crisis line before. Not because I was weak, but because I was struggling.

And struggling is not failure. It's human.

If reaching out to a hotline feels like too much right now, begin with someone you already trust:

- A friend who truly listens
- A family member who makes you feel safe
- A teacher, mentor, or coach who supports you
- A therapist, counselor, or spiritual leader

You don't have to go through this alone. There is strength in connection.

A Reminder When Things Feel Heavy

Read this slowly. Let it land.

You are not broken. You are human.

You deserve support—no matter what you're going through.

Your feelings are real, and they matter.

Help is not just for "someone else." It's for you, too.

Reaching out doesn't mean you're weak—it means you're fighting for yourself.

Even if today feels impossible, there is a future version of you who is so damn grateful you held on.

Take the next step—one breath, one call, one conversation at a time.

You are not alone. Not now. Not ever.

Glossary of Terms (aka, "What the Hell Does That Mean?")

Because sometimes you need healing decoded like it's your favorite sarcastic group chat.

Approval-Seeker Part

That one part who thinks being liked is the same as being safe.

It'll nod, smile, and volunteer for emotional labor you didn't sign up for—all to avoid conflict and rejection. It's not weak. It's just tired of being misunderstood.

Backslide

When you trip into an old pattern and your inner critic throws a party.

Doesn't mean you're broken. Means you're human. Healing isn't linear—it's a drunk toddler on a spiral staircase.

Brainspotting

Therapy that finds the trauma your words can't reach.

Looks weird. Works wonders. You stare at a fixed spot, and your brain goes all "CSI" on locked-away pain. Think of it as EMDR's quieter cousin with an attitude.

C-PTSD (Complex PTSD)

Not just one big trauma—death by a thousand emotional cuts.

Chronic, relational, hard-to-spot-but-hard-to-ignore kind of pain. Think: long-term emotional neglect, gaslighting, and growing up feeling like your feelings were "too much."

Circular Conversation

A conversational cul-de-sac where clarity goes to die.

You think you're resolving conflict. You're actually running laps around accountability. Often fueled by deflection, over-explaining, and low-key existential dread.

Deflection

When someone dodges accountability like it's dodgeball at an awkward family reunion.

Instead of owning impact, they shift focus to how you said it, how they feel about it, or how you should have said it differently. Spoiler: that's not growth—it's avoidance with a thesaurus.

Dialectical Behavior Therapy (DBT)

The emotional Swiss Army knife for people with big feelings and bad coping tools.

Helps you hold two things at once—like "I'm doing my best" *and* "I still need to do better." Great for building distress tolerance when your nervous system's on fire.

Emotional Outsourcing

When someone tries to make their healing your job.

Not the same as vulnerability. This is when their discomfort becomes your to-do list, and your boundary becomes their blame.

Emotional CPR

The script your nervous system writes when it's flatlined from being ignored too long.

It's what you do when you come back to life—slowly, shakily, and maybe with a little side-eye.

Fight / Flight / Freeze / Fawn

Your trauma's default settings.

Fight = anger outbursts. Flight = avoidance. Freeze = shutdown. Fawn = people-pleasing. These aren't choices. They're survival reflexes wearing grown-up clothes.

Glass Box Part

A teenage version of you screaming behind soundproof glass, wondering if anyone hears her.

IFS metaphor for that invisible, unheard part of you that eventually gave up trying to explain. Spoiler: She still needs you to hear her.

Healing Isn't a Glow-Up

It's a demolition followed by a rebuild with no damn blueprint.

It's messy, nonlinear, and probably involves crying in the car. But it's also how you finally stop living on autopilot.

Intent vs. Impact

Just because you didn't mean to step on someone's foot doesn't mean it didn't hurt.

Intent is about motive. Impact is about outcome. Growth means owning both without making it a debate club.

Internal Family Systems (IFS)

Your internal chaos explained like a dysfunctional family sitcom.

Everyone's got parts: the scared one, the fixer, the rage monster, the ghoster. IFS helps you meet them, lead them, and stop letting them run the damn show.

Jenga Part

The over-responsible manager who holds the whole tower together—and lives in fear of it collapsing.

This is the part that keeps the calendar, the groceries, the emotional regulation, the peace... until it burns out and rage-quits life.

Narrative Therapy

Rewriting the story so your trauma doesn't get the last word.

You're not the villain or the victim. You're the narrator—and you get to revise the plot.

Over-Explaining

What happens when you feel unsafe but still want to be understood.

You're not long-winded. You're trying to make sure they don't misunderstand, blame, or abandon you. But clarity doesn't require overexposure.

Parts Work

Therapy where you stop asking "What's wrong with me?" and start asking "Which part just took over?"

You're not broken. You're blended. And healing means learning who's driving—and who just hijacked the wheel.

Relational Life Therapy (RLT)

Where accountability stops being a threat and starts being intimacy.

Less "who's right," more "how are we harming each other, and what would repair actually look like?" Expect brutal honesty with a side of compassion.

Self-Loyalty

When you stop betraying yourself to keep the peace.

It's not selfish—it's sacred. And it's the first step in building trust with the part of you that's always watching.

Somatic Work

Healing that starts in the body, not the brain.

Because you can't logic your way out of trauma stored in your shoulders, your gut, or your jaw. Sometimes healing sounds like a yawn or feels like a deep exhale.

Trauma Bond

When your nervous system mistakes survival for love.

Not loyalty. Not connection. Just a tangle of fear, guilt, and unmet needs dressed up as intimacy.

Unhealed Trigger Trap

The moment when your old wounds start answering the phone instead of you.

You're not overreacting. You're reacting from the version of you that still thinks the threat is current.

Endnotes: Because Apparently That's What We're Calling This

Spoiler: there aren't any.

Surprise! There are no endnotes.

And no, that wasn't an oversight—it was a choice. A deliberate, eyes-wide-open, *"I'm not writing a research paper"* kind of choice.

I didn't want to interrupt the rhythm of this book with citations or footnotes every time I referenced a trauma response or dropped a therapy term. This wasn't written to impress academics—it was written to connect with actual humans trying to untangle real-life wreckage. And if you've made it this far, I'm guessing you didn't come here for APA formatting.

Giving Credit Where It's Due

Because healing language has a lineage.

Even though I didn't cite every concept inline, I want to be clear that a lot of the frameworks I wove throughout this book—like Internal Family Systems (IFS), Dialectical Behavior Therapy (DBT), attachment theory, nervous system regulation, and trauma-informed healing—come from brilliant minds who've done the research, built the scaffolding, and helped people like me make sense of our inner chaos.

So, here's to the giants whose work carried this book on its back:

- **Dr. Richard Schwartz**, who created Internal Family Systems and

252

taught us there are *no bad parts*.

- **Dr. Marsha Linehan**, who developed DBT and gave people a way to build emotional skills instead of just white-knuckling life.
- **Stephen Porges**, whose Polyvagal Theory changed how we understand the nervous system and safety.
- **Dr. Bessel van der Kolk**, who made *The Body Keeps the Score* a household phrase (and a wake-up call).
- **Dr. Bruce Perry, Peter Levine, Deb Dana**, and others who've translated trauma science into something people can actually use.
- **Dr. John Bowlby**, who laid the groundwork for attachment theory—because let's be honest, most of us are still trying to figure out how to feel safe in relationships without turning into a ghost or a barnacle.
- **Dr. Brené Brown**, whose work on shame, vulnerability, and whole-hearted living gave people permission to be messy and still worthy—and helped a lot of us stop mistaking perfectionism for protection.

This book wasn't built in a vacuum. It's a remix of lived experience, therapeutic wisdom, and a whole lot of trial-and-error healing. I integrated these ideas through years of therapy, studying psychology, unlearning generational patterns, and choosing not to emotionally self-destruct (most days). If something resonated with you deeply, chances are it has roots in something larger than just my story—and if you want to go find the source, I genuinely encourage it.

Healing isn't about reinventing the wheel. It's about finding what works and making it yours.

Bonus Reading List

For the nerdy, the skeptical, and the chronically curious.

No gatekeeping here. If you want to dig deeper into the stuff that shaped this book, these are the real ones. They're not all breezy reads, but they're worth your time. Think of this as your unofficial healing syllabus—with no quizzes, no grades, and full permission to skip around.

Psychology, Trauma & the Body

- **The Body Keeps the Score** by Bessel van der Kolk
  (Yes, it's dense. Yes, it's foundational. No, you don't have to read it cover to cover.)
- **Waking the Tiger: Healing Trauma** by Peter Levine
  (Somatic work explained without needing a neuroscience degree.)
- **What Happened to You?** by Oprah Winfrey & Dr. Bruce Perry
  (Conversation-style breakdown of trauma and brain development—surprisingly digestible.)
- **The Rewired Brain** by Dr. Ski Chilton
  (For when your survival patterns feel hardwired and you're ready to reprogram.)

Parts Work & Inner Healing

- **No Bad Parts** by Dr. Richard Schwartz
  (IFS 101 straight from the source. Also: the title alone is a healing mantra.)
- **Self-Therapy** by Jay Earley
  (A practical guide to using IFS without needing a therapist in your pocket.)
- **You Are the One You've Been Waiting For** by Dr. Richard Schwartz
  (IFS meets relationships. Get ready to cringe at your patterns—in a good way.)

Boundaries, Shame, and Emotional Resilience

- **The Gifts of Imperfection** by Brené Brown
  (Still the gold standard for people learning to stop performing their worth.)
- **I Thought It Was Just Me (But It Isn't)** by Brené Brown
  (Shame resilience, emotional honesty, and the radical reminder that

you're not broken—just human.)
- **Set Boundaries, Find Peace** by Nedra Glover Tawwab
  (Direct, practical, and actually usable in real life.)
- **Adult Children of Emotionally Immature Parents** by Lindsay C. Gibson
  (If your childhood still echoes in your adult relationships, read this.)

For the ADHD Brains, Cynical Hearts, and Burned-Out Overthinkers

- **How to Keep House While Drowning** by KC Davis
  (Shame-free, executive dysfunction-friendly, and refreshingly kind.)
- **Unmasking Autism** by Devon Price
  (Especially relevant if you've ever asked yourself, *"Wait... is it trauma or neurodivergence?"*)
- **The Subtle Art of Not Giving a F*ck** by Mark Manson
  (Cynical but insightful. Think of it as your tough-love friend who also reads philosophy.)

For Therapists Reading This

I see you. I appreciate you. Please don't come at me for my lack of citations.

First of all, thank you. If you're a therapist who picked up this book—whether out of curiosity, professional interest, or because one of your clients quoted something from it in session—I see you.

I know it can be a little disorienting to read a book that throws around therapy lingo like confetti without formal sourcing, clinical distancing, or the occasional *"in this author's opinion."* But this book wasn't written to be diagnostic—it was written to be relatable. A bridge between theory and lived experience. Between your world and your client's.

You'll probably recognize traces of IFS, DBT, somatic work, attachment theory, and parts language all over these pages. That's intentional. I've spent years immersed in this work—not as a clinician, but as someone who's had to live inside a nervous system shaped by trauma. I wanted to speak the language that so many clients feel but can't always articulate. The messy middle between *"I know better"* and *"I still can't stop spiraling."*

If anything in here helps you understand your clients better, or gives them language they didn't have before—mission accomplished. And if you ever want to recommend this book to a client, just know they won't be reading it through a clinical lens. They'll be seeing themselves in the margins. That's the whole point.

If you're looking for companion resources? Brené Brown's books (*The Gifts of Imperfection, I Thought It Was Just Me*) make great companion reads for clients working through shame, vulnerability, and self-worth alongside the deeper trauma work.

Thanks for the work you do. The world needs it. And I'm rooting for you, too.

Conclusion

Because healing doesn't mean you'll never lose your sh*t again.

Let's be clear: healing doesn't mean you'll never fall apart. It means that when you do, you'll know what it is, why it's happening, and how to come back from it—without shame spiraling into oblivion.

You've made it through this book—which means you've faced some hard truths, probably argued with a few of them, and maybe even found pieces of yourself you forgot you were allowed to keep. That's not small. That's not soft. That's sacred.

This isn't the end of your healing journey. It's a checkpoint. A pause to breathe, regroup, and remember that you don't have to start over every time you fall apart. You're not broken. You're rebuilding. And sometimes that means collapsing a few more walls before you find what's underneath.

You've got tools now. You've met your parts. You've questioned your patterns. You've stared fear in the face and called it out for the manipulative little liar it is. That's not just healing—that's power.

So when the next wave hits (because it will), don't panic. Don't backslide into the lie that you're too much, too messy, or too late. Pull out a tool, take a breath, and remember:

You're not who you were when you started this book.

And that's the whole damn point.

Fine, I'll keep going.

257

About the Author

Trauma nerd. Creative powerhouse. Emotional truth-teller in a hoodie.

Whitney Stone is a trauma nerd, creative powerhouse, and recovering over-explainer who writes like your sarcastic best friend and emotionally intelligent therapist had a baby. After spending years stuck in survival mode, masking pain with productivity, and gaslighting herself better than anyone else ever could, she finally decided to stop faking fine and figure out what healing actually looked like in real life.

She's not a licensed therapist (*yet*), but don't let that fool you—Whitney has spent years immersed in the worlds of Internal Family Systems (IFS), Dialectical Behavior Therapy (DBT), attachment theory, and nervous system regulation. All while raising a neurodivergent teen *and* a fiercely insightful teenage daughter, running a creative business, and occasionally remembering to eat lunch. Her work is rooted in lived experience, obsessive research, and a refusal to pretend that healing has to look pretty to be real.

When she's not writing, Whitney is behind the camera photographing high school seniors and sporting events through her business, Two Stones Photography. She also finds joy in sublimation crafting (because healing comes in layers—and polyester), watching her kids become their favorite selves, and having unexpectedly deep car conversations about life, fear, and memes.

She lives in small-town Minnesota with her husband, two kids, and a crew of boxers and a golden retriever who are absolutely convinced they're emotional support animals—and honestly, they're not wrong.